First International Workshop on Optimization Techniques for Human Language Technology

Held at the 24th International Conference on Computational Linguistics (COLING 2012)

Mumbai, India
9 December 2012

Editors:

Pushpak Bhattacharyya
Asif Ekbal
Sriparna Saha
Mark Johnson
Diego Molla-Aliod
Mark Dras

ISBN: 978-1-62748-361-2

Printed from e-media with permission by:

Curran Associates, Inc.
57 Morehouse Lane
Red Hook, NY 12571

Some format issues inherent in the e-media version may also appear in this print version.

Printed by Curran Associates, Inc. (2013)

Association for Computational Linguistics
209 N. Eighth Street
Stroudsburg, Pennsylvania 18360

Phone: 1-570-476-8006
Fax: 1-570-476-0860

acl@aclweb.org

Additional copies of this publication are available from:

Curran Associates, Inc.
57 Morehouse Lane
Red Hook, NY 12571 USA
Phone: 845-758-0400
Fax: 845-758-2634
Email: curran@proceedings.com
Web: www.proceedings.com

Preface

In decision science, optimization is quite an obvious and important tool. Depending on the number of objectives, the optimization technique can be single or multiobjective. We encounter numerous real life scenarios where multiple objectives need to be satisfied in the course of optimization. Finding a single solution in such cases is very difficult, if not impossible. In such problems, referred to as multiobjective optimization problems (MOOPs), it may also happen that optimizing one objective leads to some unacceptably low value of the other objective(s). Evolutionary algorithms and simulated annealing, from the family of meta-heuristic search and optimization techniques, have shown promise in solving complex single as well as multiobjective optimization problems in a wide variety of domains.

Language technology and/or Natural language processing (NLP) is an interdisciplinary field of computer science and linguistics concerned with the interactions between computers and human (natural) languages. It is a branch of artificial intelligence. In theory, NLP is a very attractive method of human-computer interaction. Natural language understanding is sometimes referred to as an AI-complete problem because it seems to require extensive knowledge about the outside world and the ability to manipulate it. Modern NLP algorithms are grounded in machine learning, especially statistical machine learning. Research into modern statistical NLP algorithms requires an understanding of a number of disparate fields, including linguistics, computer science, and statistics. Major tasks in NLP include Automatic summarization, Coreference resolution, Named Entity Recognition, Machine translation, Machine transliteration, Natural language generation, Natural language understanding, Morphological segmentation, Part-of-Speech tagging, Question answering, Sentiment analysis, Speech segmentation, Word sense disambiguation, Information retrieval etc.

In each of the above mentioned tasks, there are various metrics that we often need to optimize to get the reasonable performance. Many evaluation metrics have been proposed for solving different problems of NLP. For example, in Information retrieval, it is often necessary to optimize the recall and precision parameters. In automatic summarization, it is desired to optimize different objective functions like similarity to user query, ROUGE metric, important sentence score, difference in length between the scored sentence and the desired sentence and many others. Other examples of optimization in NLP include parsing, machine translation, and computational models of language acquisition.

This volume contains papers accepted for presentation at the First International Workshop on Optimization Techniques for Human Language Technology. The event took place on December 9, 2012, in Mumbai, India, as a workshop in COLING 2012, the 24th International Conference on Computational Linguistics. The workshop was a starting platform to explore the possibilities of interdisciplinary research that will focus on developing optimisation based methods within the context of human language technology.

Eight papers were accepted for presentation, based on the careful reviews of a panel of international experts in various areas related to the workshop goals. Our sincere thanks to all the reviewers for their thoughtful reviews.

We would like to thank Prof. Aravind K. Joshi, University of Pennsylvania for his invited speech on "Complexity of Parse representations, Parsing complexity, Side Information: Relevance to Optimization?"

We would also like to thank the Australia-India Strategic Research Fund (AISRF) for sponsoring the workshop.

Asif Ekbal, Pushpak Bhattacharyya, Sriparna Saha,
Mark Johnson, Diego Molla, Mark Dras.
December 2012.

Organizers:

Asif Ekbal (Indian Institute of Technology Patna, Bihar, India) (Chair)
Pushpak Bhattacharyya (Indian Institute of Technology Bombay, India)
Sriparna Saha (Indian Institute of Technology Patna, India)
Mark Johnson (Department of Computing, Macquarie University, Australia)
Diego Molla (Macquarie University, Australia)
Mark Dras (Macquarie University, Australia)

Program Committee:

Ramiz M. Aliguliyev (Azerbaijan National Academy of Sciences, Azerbaijan)
Timothy Baldwin (University of Melbourne, Australia)
Sivaji Bandyopadhyay (Jadavpur University, India)
Malay Bhattacharyya (Kalyani University, India)
Pushpak Bhattacharyya (Indian Institute of Technology Bombay, India)
Benjamin Boerschingen (Macquarie University, Australia)
Niladri Chatterjee (IIT Delhi)
Monojit Choudhury (Microsoft Research India)
Walter Daelemans (University of Antwerp)
Gaël Harry Dias (University of Caen Basse-Normadie, France)
Soumyajit Dey (Indian Institute of Technology Patna, India)
Patrick Saint-Dizier (Institut de Recherches en Informatique de Toulouse)
Mark Dras (Macquarie University, Australia)
Lan Du (Macquarie University, Australia)
Asif Ekbal (Indian Institute of Technology Patna, Bihar, India) (Chair)
Alexander Gelbukh (National Polytechnic Institute (IPN), Mexico)
Veronique Hoste (University College Ghent)
Jagadeesh Jagarlamudi (University of Maryland College Park, USA)
Mark Johnson (Department of Computing, Macquarie University, Australia)
Nitin Indurkya (University of New South Wales, Australia)
Zornitsa Kozareva (Information Sciences Institute / University of Southern California, USA)
A Kumaran (Microsoft Research India)
Pabitra Mitra (Indian Institute of Technology Kharagpur, India)
Diego Molla (Macquarie University, Australia)
Samrat Mondal (Indian Institute of Technology Patna, India)
Anirban Mukhopadhyay (Kalyani University, India)
Massimo Poesio (University of Trento, Italy)
Sriparna Saha (Indian Institute of Technology Patna, India)
Ashok Singh Sairam (Indian Institute of Technology Patna)
Soumi Sengupta (Indian Statistical Institute Kolkata, India)
Jyoti Prakash Singh (National Institute of Technology Patna, India)
Olga Uryupina (University of Trento, Italy)
Sriram Venkatapathy (Xerox Research Centre Europe)
Jose Luis Vicedo (University of Alicante, Spain)

Invited Speaker:

Aravind K. Joshi (University of Pennsylvania, USA)

Workshop chairs:
Pushpak Bhattacharyya, Asif Ekbal, Sriparna Saha, Mark Johnson, Diego Molla-Aliod and Mark Dras

Diamond sponsors

Tata Consultancy Services
Linguistic Data Consortium for Indian Languages (LDC-IL)

Gold Sponsors

Microsoft Research
Beijing Baidu Netcon Science Technology Co. Ltd.

Silver sponsors

IBM, India Private Limited
Crimson Interactive Pvt. Ltd.
Yahoo
Easy Transcription & Software Pvt. Ltd.

Table of Contents

First International Workshop on Optimization Techniques for Human Language Technology

Program

Sunday, 9 December 2012

09:45	Start
10:00–11:00	**Invited Talk:** *Complexity of Parse representations, Parsing complexity, Side Information: Relevance to Optimization?* Aravind K. Joshi, University of Pennsylvania
	Session 1
11:00–11:30	*BioPOS: Biologically Inspired Algorithms for POS Tagging* Ana Paula Silva, Arlindo Silva and Irene Rodrigues
11:30–12:00	Tea break
	Session 2
12:00–12:30	*Optimization for Efficient Determination of Chunk in Automatic Evaluation for Machine Translation* Hiroshi Echizen'ya, Kenji Araki and Eduard Hovy
12:30–13:00	*Optimizing Transliteration for Hindi/Marathi to English Using only Two Weights* Manikrao Dhore, Shantanu Dixit and Ruchi Dhore
13:00–13:30	*Selection of Discriminative Features for Translation Texts* Kuo-Ming Tang, Chien-Kang Huang and Chia-Ming Lee
13:30–14:30	Lunch
	Session 3
14:30–15:00	*Semi-supervised Learning of Naive Bayes Classifier with feature constraints* Nagesh Bhattu Sristy and D.V.L.N Somayajulu
15:00–15:30	*Optimization and Sampling for NLP from a Unified Viewpoint* Marc Dymetman, Guillaume Bouchard and Simon Carter
15:30–16:00	*Iterative Chinese Bi-gram Term Extraction Using Machine-learning Classification Approach* Chia-Ming Lee, Chien-Kang Huang and Kuo-Ming Tang
16:00–16:30	*Parameter estimation under uncertainty with Simulated Annealing applied to an ant colony based probabilistic WSD algorithm* Andon Tchechmedjiev, Jérôme Goulian, Didier Schwab and Gilles Sérasset
16:30	Workshop end

BioPOS: Biologically Inspired Algorithms for POS Tagging

Ana Paula Silva[1] *Arlindo Silva*[1] *IreneRodrigues*[2]
(1) Polytechnic Institute of Castelo Branco, Portugal
(2) University of Evora, Portugal
dorian@ipcb.pt, arlindo@ipcb.pt, ipr@uevora.pt

ABSTRACT
In this paper we present a new biologically inspired approach to the part-of-speech tagging problem, based on particle swarm optimization. As far as we know this is the first attempt of solving this problem using swarm intelligence. We divided the part-of-speech problem into two subproblems. The first concerns the way of automatically extracting disambiguation rules from an annotated corpus. The second is related with how to apply these rules to perform the automatic tagging. We tackled both problems with particle swarm optimization. We tested our approach using two different corpora of English language and also a Portuguese corpus. The accuracy obtained on both languages is comparable to the best results previously published, including other evolutionary approaches.

KEYWORDS: Part-of-speech Tagging, Particle Swarm Optimization, Disambiguation Rules, Natural Language Processing.

Proceedings of the First International Workshop on Optimization Techniques for Human Language Technology, pages 1–16,
COLING 2012, Mumbai, December 2012.

1 Introduction

The part-of-speech (POS) tagging is a fundamental step for the execution of other natural language processing (NLP) tasks, like phrase chunking, parsing, named entity recognition, machine translation, information retrieval, speech recognition, etc. It is the process of classifying words according to the roles they assume in a sentence. The task is not straightforward because words in most languages can assume different roles in a sentence, depending on how they are used. Those roles are normally designated by part-of-speech tags or word classes, such as nouns, verbs, adjectives and adverbs.

The role of a word in a sentence is determined by it's surrounding words (context). For instance, the word *fish* can assume the function of a **verb**, "Men like to fish.", or a **noun**, "I like smoked fish", depending on how we choose to use it on a sentence. This means that in order to assign to each word of a sentence its correct tag, we have to consider the context in which each word appears. However, each of the words belonging to a word's context can also be used in different ways, and that means that in order to solve the problem we need some type of disambiguation mechanism.

Traditionally, there are two groups of methods used to tackle this task, with respect to the information model used. The first group is based on statistical data concerning the different context possibilities for a word (stochastic taggers) (Brants, 2000; Araujo, 2002, 2004, 2007; Araujo et al., 2004; Alba et al., 2006), while the second group is based on rules that capture the language properties and are used to improve tagging accuracy (Brill, 1995; Wilson and Heywood, 2005; Nogueira Dos Santos et al., 2008).

The simplest stochastic tagger, called unigram tagger, takes only into account the word itself. It assigns the tag that is most likely for one particular token. The tagger works like a simple lookup tagger, assigning to each word the most common tag for that word in the training corpus. To do that, the learning process just counts, for each word, the number of times it appears with each of the possible tags. An n-gram tagger is a generalization of a unigram tagger, whose context is the current word together with the part-of-speech tags of the n-1 preceding tokens. In this case, the training step saves, for each possible tag, the number of times it appears in every different context presented on the training corpus. Since the surrounding words can also have various possibilities of classification, it is necessary to use a statistical model that allows the selection of the best choices for marking the entire sequence, according to the model. Most of the stochastic taggers are based on hidden Markov models, and, because of that, a word's context consists only in the tags of the words that precede it. However, more recently, other taggers have emerged that, although based on stochastic information, have used different models that make possible to consider different context shapes.

One of the most popular taggers based on rules is the one proposed by Brill (Brill, 1995). Brill's rules are usually called transformation rules. The system can be divided into two main components: a list of transformation rules patterns for error correction, and a learning system. The transformation patterns are handmade and provided to the learning algorithm, which will instantiate and order them. The search is made in a greedy fashion. The result is an ordered set of transformation rules, which is then used to perform the tagging. These rules are meant to correct mistakes in a pre-tagged text, usually achieved by a baseline system that marks each word with its most common tag. They are applied in a iterative way until no rule can be fired.

As already observed, the only information an n-gram tagger considers from prior context is the tags, even though words themselves might be a useful source of information. It is simply impractical for n-gram models to be conditioned by the context words themselves (and not only their tags). On the other hand, Brill's approach allows the inclusion of other type of information besides the context. In fact, the author also used the learning algorithm to achieve a set of lexicalized transformation rules, that includes not only the tags but the words themselves.

There are also some other aspects that can be used to determine a word's category beside it's context in a sentence (Steven Bird and Loper, 2009). The internal structure of a word may give useful clues as to the word's class. For example, in the English language, *-ness* is a suffix that combines with an adjective to produce a noun, e.g., *happy* → *happiness, ill* → *illness*. Therefore, if we encounter a word that ends in *-ness*, it is very likely to be a noun. Similarly, *-ing* is a suffix that is most commonly associated with gerunds, like *walking, talking, thinking, listening*. We also might guess that any word ending in *-ed* is the past participle of a verb, and any word ending with *'s* is a possessive noun.

More recently, several evolutionary approaches have been proposed to solve the tagging problem. These approaches can also be divided by the type of information used to solve the problem, statistical information (Araujo, 2002, 2004, 2007; Araujo et al., 2004; Alba et al., 2006), and rule-based information (Wilson and Heywood, 2005).

Although there is a substantial amount of work about POS tagging applied to the English language, there are, comparatively, a small number of attempts to approach the problem using the Portuguese language. One of the main reasons is the limited number of resources that exist for it. Nevertheless, we can find some work where several of the existing techniques used to solve the POS tagging are tested on the Portuguese language: transformation based learning (Aires et al., 2000), Markov models (Kepler and Finger, 2006), entropy guided transformation learning (Nogueira Dos Santos et al., 2008).

One of the problems of the stochastic taggers, is that they tend to be dependent of the domain in which they are trained. Also, the information used is in the form of probabilistic values, which are less comprehensible than data presented in the form of rules, and only contemplates context information. In this work, we investigate the possibility of extracting, from an annotated corpus, a set of rules similar to classification rules, that could be used to help the decision process needed to perform the tagging. With our approach, we hope to be able to learn rules that prove to be more generic than the information used by the stochastic taggers, so that the tagger performs well in different domains. We also intend to include in these rules, together with the context information, other type of data, namely some aspects related with the word morphology. To accomplish our goals, we chose one technology that has already proven to be successful in data mining tasks, in particular in the discovery of classification rules (Sousa et al., 2004) - the particle swarm optimization (PSO) algorithm.

We also investigate the possibility of using a discrete PSO algorithm to perform the tagging, using the disambiguation rules to guide the evolution of the swarm. The problem of searching for the best tag assignments can be seen as a combinatorial optimization problem, where a solution is evaluated with the help of the disambiguation rules previously learned. We decided to test the application of swarm intelligence to this problem, since other population based algorithms, in particular genetic algorithms, have been successfully applied to many combinatorial optimization tasks. In order to evaluate the success of our approach we tested it on two different languages: English and Portuguese.

The remainder of this paper is organized as follows. In section 2, we describe the two evolutionary approaches to the POS tagging problem that we think are the most closely related to the work reported in this paper. In section 3, we present the general idea behind particle swarm optimization. The particle swarm optimization algorithm for disambiguation rules discovery is outlined in section 4 and the POS-Tagger in section 5. The experimental results are presented in section 6, and finally, in section 7, we make some concluding remarks.

2 Previous Work

In this section we present a brief description of the two approaches more closely related to our work, in that both of them use evolutionary algorithms to tackle some aspect of the part-of-speech problem. We begin with the part-of speech tagger developed by Wilson (Wilson and Heywood, 2005), and then we discuss the evolutionary tagger developed by Araujo (Araujo, 2002).

2.1 Wilson's Tagger

The system proposed in (Wilson and Heywood, 2005) is an evolutionary version of the Brill's tagging system (Brill, 1995) based on non lexical transformation rules. The authors propose a genetic algorithm to learn the rewrite rules, instead of the greedy algorithm described by Brill.

In the genetic algorithm presented, an individual of the population is a list of rewrite rules. The chosen representation was a fixed-length binary representation, in which each individual represents a set of 378 rules. The initial order of the rules is determined randomly. During the evolutionary process the order can be changed by the recombination operator.

Each rule is a sequence of 48 bits.The initial population is randomly generated. Each individual represents an ordered collection of rules that potentially solves the problem of marking the Wall Street Journal corpus. Each rule takes in consideration the tags of the three words to the left and to the right of the current word. An extra bit is used for each of the context elements, to indicate if that element should be considered in the rule. Thus the leftmost bit in the string indicates whether the triggering environment involves examining the third tag back from the target tag position. The next six bits indicate what tag should be sought in that position by using the integer equivalent of the binary representation.

The six bits map onto a 45 part-of-speech tags from the Penn Treebank, and if the integer equivalent of the six bits exceeds 45, the tag is considered to be the remainder of the integer division by 45. The next bit indicates whether to examine the second tag back. What tag to look for there is indicated by the next six bits. The same interpretation is made for the next seven bits, considering the tag of the previous word. The next six bits indicate what tag is to replace that of the target position. The tags sough (and wether or not they should be sough) in the three positions following the target are given by the following 21 bits. The interpretation is the same as that described for the positions previous to the target position.

The performance of an individual is given by the accuracy of the tagging achieved with the set of rules it represents. The experimental conditions used by Wilson attempt to follow the ones used by Brill nonlexicalized tagger. They used only nonlexicalized rules and each individual is composed by 378 rules. In each rule the tags located 3 positions previous to the target and 3 positions following the target position, are examined. They used a subset of the Pen Treebank corpus, composed of 600000 words to learn the rules. A closed vocabulary assumption was adopted. The best result achieved in the training corpus obtained an accuracy of 89.8%. There is no reference to experiments made in a separate test set with the best set of rules evolved by the evolutionary algorithm.

2.2 Araujo's Tagger

The system proposed in (Araujo, 2002) uses an evolutionary algorithm to perform the tagging. In order to tag the words of a text, the algorithm must be run separately for each sentence of the text. In the proposed algorithm, each individual in the population represents a candidate solution to the tagging problem. Thus, each individual comprises a chromosome composed by as many genes as the number of words of the sentence to tag. Each gene refers to the sentence word in the same position, i.e. the gene g_i contains information concerning the word, w_i of the sentence to tag. This information includes a candidate tag for the word, and data related with the context of that part-of-speech. The context information is obtained in an initial step and is stored as a table - the training table. For each part-of-speech of the training corpus the number of times each of one appears in every possible context was counted. The authors considered contexts that include tags appearing before and after a certain part-of-speech. Experiments with different sizes of context were coducted.

The performance of a particular chromosome was measured using a fitness function defined as the sum of the evaluation of each of the genes that compose the chromosome. A gene is evaluated based on the statistical information collected and stored in the training table. The value obtained is an estimative of the accuracy of the tag proposed by the gene for a particular word in the sentence.

The evolutionary process aims to choose, for a particular sentence, the sequence of tags that maximize the total probability, based on the statistical data obtained previously. The authors conclude that the corpus used for training the system has a great influence on the algorithm performance, and state that a corpus which proves to be a good sample of the language should be used. However, that is not always possible, since in most cases the corpora available are specific to a particular domain.

The results presented were achieved with the Brown corpus. The best results presented, using a test set of 2500 words, were below 95.5%.

3 Particle Swarm Optimization

PSO is inspired in the intelligent behavior of agents as part of an experience sharing community, as opposed to an isolated individual reactive response to the environment. The adaptive culture model (Kennedy and Eberhart, 2001), which is PSO's framing theory, states that the process of cultural adaptation is rooted into three principles: evaluate, compare and imitate. Evaluation is the capacity to qualify environmental stimuli and the *sine qua non* condition to social learning. Evaluation itself is both useless and impossible without the ability to compare; all of our metrics are but a comparison to a well-known unit and a single value becomes pointless without the values of it peers. At last, imitation is the rawest form of experience sharing from the receiver's standpoint; it involves not only observation but also realization of purpose and timing adequacy.

In PSO algorithms, a particle decides where to move next, considering its own experience, which is the memory of its best past position, and the experience of its most successful neighbor. There may be different concepts and values for neighborhood; it can be seen as spatial neighborhood where it is determined by the Euclidean distance between the positions of two particles, or as a sociometric neighborhood (e.g.: the index position in the storing array). Although some actions differ from one variant of PSO to the other, the common pseudo-code for PSO is as follows:

The output of this algorithm is the best point in the hyperspace the swarm visited. Since its introduction, the PSO algorithm has been successfully applied to problems in different areas,

Algorithm 1 Generic Particle Swarm Optimization Algorithm

```
Initiate_Swarm()
repeat
  for p= 1 to number of particles do
    Evaluate(p)
    Update_past_experience(p)
    Update_neighborhood_best(p,k)
    for d= 1 to number of Dimensions do
      Move(p,d)
    end for
  end for
until Criterion
```

including antenna design, computer graphics visualization, biomedical applications, design of electrical networks, and many others (Poli, 2008). Amongst the qualities that led to this popularity are its conceptual simplicity, ease of implementation and low computational costs. The algorithm works well with small swarms and tends to converge fast to a solution. In addition, particle swarm optimization has proven itself to be easily adaptable to new domains of application and to work well when hybridized with other approaches. There are several variants of PSO, including algorithms for discrete and continuous domains. The variant used in our work was the discrete PSO introduced by Kennedy (Kennedy and Eberhart, 2001).

3.1 Discrete Swarm Optimization Algorithm

This variant of the PSO considers each bit as a dimension, with 2 possible values 0 or 1. Particle motion is just the toggling between these two values.

There is a velocity value(V_{id}) associated with each dimension/bit; this vale is randomly generated from a range of $[-4.0, 4.0]$ when the particle is created and iteratively updated (1) according to his previous best position (P_{id}) and the best position in the neighborhood (P_{gd}). φ_1 and φ_2 are random weights whose role is to provide diversity between individual learning and social influence.

$$V_{id}(t+1) = V_{id}(t-1) + \varphi_1(P_{id} - x_{id}(t-1)) + \varphi_2(P_{gd} - xi, d(t-1)) \tag{1}$$

To determine if a bit will toggle (2), a random number, ρ, is drawn from a uniform distribution ranging from 0 to 1, and is compared to a normalized value of the velocity associated with this dimension.

$$x_{i,d} = \begin{cases} 1 & \text{if } \rho < S(v_{id}(t)) \\ 0 & \text{otherwise} \end{cases} \tag{2}$$

The sigmoid function (3) is used here to insure that the velocity's value is kept in the range of $[0.0, 1.0]$.

$$S(v_{id}) = \frac{1}{1 + exp(-v_{id})} \tag{3}$$

4 Particle Swarm Optimization Algorithm for Disambiguation Rules Discovery

In this section we describe the use of a discrete PSO (DPSO) algorithm to discover a set of disambiguation rules, that will be used to help the optimization process necessary to solve the part-of-speech tagging problem. We will approach the problem as if we were trying to solve a classification problem, by learning a set of classification rules.

The overall structure of our approach was designed to include two nested algorithms. The innermost algorithm is the classification rule discovery algorithm. Its task is to find and return the rule which better classifies the training examples. As we said before we adopted a DPSO to perform this task. The outmost algorithm is a covering algorithm that receives the training set, divided in two sets - the set of positive examples and the set of negative examples. It then invokes the classification rule discovery algorithm to reduce this set by removing instances of the set of positive examples, that are correctly classified by the rule returned by the classification rule discovery algorithm. This process is repeated until there are no examples to classify (see algorithm 2).

Algorithm 2 Covering Algorithm

Require: SetOfPosExamples, SetOfNegExamples
Ensure: SetOfRules
  while SetOfPosExamples $\neq \emptyset$ **do**
    BestRule = DPSO(SetOfPosExamples, SetOfNegExamples)
    SetOfPosExamples = RemoveExamples(SetOfPosExamples, BestRule)
    SetOfRules = Add(SetOfRules, BestRule)
  end while

4.1 Rule Representation

Classification rules are no more than conditional clauses, involving two parts: the antecedent and the consequent. The former is the conjunction of logical tests, and the latter gives the class that applies to instances covered by this rule. These rules take the following format:
IF $attrib_a$ = val_1 AND $attrib_b$ = val_2 ..... AND $attrib_n$ = val_i THEN $class_x$.

In evolutionary rule classifier systems there are two distinct approaches to individual or particle representation: the Michigan and the Pittsburgh approaches (Freitas, 2003). In the Michigan approach each individual encodes a single rule, whereas in the Pittsburgh approach each individual encodes a set of rules. In our work, we follow the Michigan approach, and rules are coded using binary strings; each attribute is assigned with the necessary bit number to accommodate its value range. An extra bit is used to represent any value, meaning that no logical test is performed to this attribute when this bit is activated. As we stated in Introduction, our aim is to discover a set of rules that take into consideration not only context information but also information about the words' morphology.

We decided to test our approach on the English and Portuguese languages. Thereby, since the structure of the languages are different, we needed to extract disambiguation rules from a English and a Portuguese corpora. We adopted a slightly different type of rules for the two languages. For the context, we decided to consider the same information that was used in the work of Brill (Brill, 1995) and Wilson (Wilson and Heywood, 2005). Thus, we consider six attributes: the lexical categories of the third, second and first words to the left, and the lexical categories of the first, second, and third words to the right. These attributes were used for the rules of both languages. For the words' morphology information we decided to include, for the English language as well as for the Portuguese language, the following attributes: 'The word is capitalized?', 'The word is the first word of the sentence?'. In addition, for the English language, we incorporated on the rules' antecedent these attributes: 'The word ends with ***ed***?' 'The word ends with ***ing***?', 'The word ends with ***es***?' , 'The word ends with ***ould***?' , 'The word ends with ***'s***?', 'The word ends with ***s***?', 'The word has numbers or '.' and numbers?'.

The possible values for each of the first six attributes are the values of the corpus tag set from which the evolutionary algorithm will extract the rules. This set will depend on the annotated corpus used, since the set of used labels will vary for different annotated corpora. The maximum number of tags on the tag sets we used was 29, so we used six bits to represent each attribute. The first bit indicates whether the attribute should or should not be considered, and the following five bits represent the assumed value of the attribute in question. We adopted a table of n entries, to store the tag set, with n representing the cardinality of the set, and used the binary value represented by five bits to index this table. If the value exceeds the number n, we used the remainder of the division by n.

The remaining k attributes were encoded by $2 \times k$ bits, two bits for each of the k attributes. In the same way, the first bit indicates if the attribute should, or shouldn't be considered and the second bit, indicates whether the property is, or is not, present. In short, for the English language each particle was composed by $6 \times 6 + 2 \times 9 = 54$ bits, and for the Portuguese language each particle was made by $6 \times 6 + 2 \times 2 = 40$ bits.

In general, there are three different ways to represent the predicted class in an evolutionary algorithm (Freitas, 2003). One way is to encode it into the genome of the individual, or the particle, opening the possibility of subjecting it to evolution (de Jong et al., 1993; Greene and Smith, 1993). Another way is to associate all individuals of the population to the same class, which is never modified during the execution of the algorithm. Thus, if we are to find a set of classification rules to predict k distinct classes, we need to run the evolutionary algorithm, at least k times. In each i-th execution, the algorithm only discovers rules that predict the i-th class (Janikow, 1993). The third possibility consists in choosing the predicted class in a more or less deterministic way. The chosen class may be the one that has more representatives in the set of examples that satisfy the antecedent of the rule (Giordana and Neri, 1995), or the class that maximizes the performance of the individual (Noda et al., 1999) . We adopted the second possibility, so we didn't need to encode the rule's consequent. This choice determines that the covering algorithm needs to be ran for each tag of the tag set adopted for the experimental work.

4.2 Rule Evaluation - Establishing Reference Points

Rules must be evaluated during the training process in order to establish points of reference for the training algorithm. The rule evaluation function must not only consider instances correctly classified, but also the ones left to classify and the wrongly classified ones. The formula used to evaluate a rule, and therefore to set its quality, is expressed in equation 4. This formula penalizes a particle that represents a rule that ignores the first six attributes, which are related with the word's context, forcing it to assume a more desirable form. The others are evaluated by the well known F_β-measure. The F_β-measure can be interpreted as a weighted average of precision and recall. We used $\beta = 0.09$, which means we put more emphasis on precision than recall.

$$Q(X) = \begin{cases} F_\beta(X) & \text{if context(X) = True} \\ -1 & \text{otherwise} \end{cases} \tag{4}$$

$$context(X) = \begin{cases} True & \text{if } X \text{ tests at least one of the first six attributes} \\ False & \text{otherwise} \end{cases} \tag{5}$$

$$F_\beta(X) = (1+\beta^2) \times \frac{precision(X) \times recall(X)}{\beta^2 \times precison(X) + recall(X)} \tag{6}$$

$$precision(X) = \frac{TP}{TP + FP} \tag{7}$$

$$recall(X) = \frac{TP}{TP + FN} \tag{8}$$

where:

- TP - True Positives = number of instances covered by the rule that are correctly classified, i.e., its class matches the training target class;
- FP - False Positives = number of instances covered by the rule that are wrongly classified, i.e., its class differs from the training target class;
- FN - False Negatives = number of instances not covered by the rule, whose class matches the training target class.

4.3 Pre-processing Routines - Data Extraction

For the English language we used the Brown corpus to create the training set that we provided as input to the discrete PSO for the extraction of the disambiguation rules. The corpus used for the Portuguese language was the Mac-Morpho. For each word of both corpus we collected the values for every attribute included in the rule's antecedent, creating a specific training example. Then, for each tag of the tag set, we built a training set composed by positive and negative examples of the tag.

Usually, the set of positive (negative) examples of a class is composed by examples that do (do not) belong to that particular class. However, in our case, we are not interested in finding typical classification rules, our goal is not to solve a classification problem, we just need rules that help to choose the best tag from a set of possible tags. This set is not all the tag set, but a subset of it, usually composed by a small number of elements. When we have a word that has only one possible lexical class, the tagging is straightforward. The problematic words are the ones that are ambiguous. Thus, our training set should only include examples corresponding to ambiguous words. The building process used to define each of the training sets was the following: for each example e_i of the set of examples, with word w and tag t, if w is an ambiguous word, with S the set of all its possible tags, then put e_i in the set of positive examples of tag t, and put e_i in the set of negative examples of all the tags in S, except t.

4.4 Experimental Work

We developed our system in Python and used the resources available on the NLTK (Natural Language Toolkit) package in our experiences. The NLTK package provides, for the English language, among others, the Brown corpus and a sample of 10% of the Wall Street Journal (WSJ) corpus of the Penn Treebank. These corpora are the most frequently used to test taggers' performances on the English language and the ones used in the approaches we mentioned earlier. The Mac-Morpho corpus is also available for the Portuguese language.

4.4.1 English Language

The corpus used for the extraction of the disambiguation rules for the English language was the Brown corpus. Tagged corpora use many different conventions for tagging words. This means that the tag sets vary from corpus to corpus. Besides, our approach determines that, to extract the disambiguation rules from a set of annotated texts, we need to run our algorithm for each of the tags belonging to the tag set. However, our intention was to test the rules extracted from the Brown corpus on a different corpus of the same language, namely the WSJ corpus. Since these corpora have different tag sets we will not be able to measure the performance of our tagger on the WSJ corpus with the rules found on the Brown corpus. To avoid this, we decided to use the *simplify_tags=True* option of the *tagged_sentence* module of NLTK corpus readers. When this option is set to *True*, NLTK converts the respective tag set of the Brown and WSJ corpora to a uniform simplified tag set, composed by 29 tags. This simplified tag set establishes the set of classes we use in our algorithm for the English language. We ran the covering algorithm for each one of the classes that had ambiguous words in the brown corpus.

We processed the Brown corpus and, for each word found, we built the correspondent instance. The total number of examples extracted from the corpus equals 929286. We used 5 subsets of this set (with different cardinality) to conduct our experiments We used sets of size: 30000, 40000, 50000, 60000, 70000. The examples were taken from the beginning of the corpus. For each subset adopted, we built the sets of positive and negative examples for each ambiguous tag, using the process described in the previous section. We used a compacted representation of the examples: for each different example we saved the number of times it appears in the set

The discrete PSO algorithm was run with a swarm of 20 particles for a maximum of 200 generations. These values were established after some preliminary experiments. We ran the algorithm 4 times for each of the sets, and tested the resulting rules by providing them to the PSO-Tagger, which we will describe next. The set that produced the best results on the PSO-Tagger was the one with 50000 tokens. The discovery algorithm found a total number of 3385 rules for this set.

4.4.2 Portuguese Language

Like we said before, we used the Mac-Morpho corpus to extract the disambiguation rules for the Portuguese language. This corpus contains 1.2 million manually tagged words. Its tag set contains 22 POS tags and 10 more tags that represent additional semantics aspects. We carried out our experiments using only the 22 POS tags.

We processed the Mac-Morpho corpus in much the same way we processed the Brown corpus. But in this case we used the first 60% of the Mac-Morpho sentences to build the examples used to define the sets of positive and negative examples for each of the tags of the tag set used in this corpus. A compacted representation was also used. Notwithstanding, to reduce the number of examples of each set, we eliminated the ones that only appeared one, two or three times, depending on the cardinality of the positive and negative sets. Between positive and negative examples, we considered a total of 107200 different examples . We ran the discrete PSO algorithm with 20 particles during 200 generations. The set of rules found that provided the best tagging had 5988 rules.

5 PSO-Tagger

The PSO-Tagger was designed to receive as inputs a sentence, a set of disambiguation rules and a dictionary. The returned output is the input sentence with each of its words marked with the correct POS tag. The discrete PSO algorithm evolves a swarm of particles, that encode, each of them, a sequence of tags to mark the ambiguous words of the input sentence. Since we adopted the discrete version of the PSO algorithm, we used a binary representation for the particles. To encode each of the tags belonging to the tag set, used in the experimental work, we used a string of 5 bits. Therefore, a particle that proposes a tagging for a sentence with n ambiguous words will be represented by $n \times 5$ bits.

5.1 Representation

Each five bits of a particle encode a integer number that indexes a table with as much entries as the possible tags for the correspondent ambiguous word. If the integer number given by the binary string exceeds the table size, we use as index the remainder of the division by the table size value. As we said before, we intend to use the disambiguation rules, found by the discovery algorithm described in the previous section, to guide the evolution of the swarm particles. Since these rules have six attributes related with the word context, and other k attributes concerning morphological properties of the words, we need to build, from the input sentence and from the tags proposed by the particles, the values of each one of the attributes contemplated in the rules' antecedents.

Although the particles only propose tags for the ambiguous words, the tags of the unambiguous ones will be needed to extract the attributes' values. Thus, before optimization begins, the discrete PSO marks each of these words with the correspondent tag, by simple input dictionary lookup. So a particle completes the previous lookup based tagging, and provides a full marked sentence. This sentence can then be used to extract a set of instances composed by the $6+k$ attributes, so that the disambiguation rules can be applied. This way, each pair w_i/t_i in the full annotated sentence results in a $(6+k+1)$-tuple made by the $6+k$ attributes and by t_i. The English disambiguation rules had $k=9$, and the Portuguese disambiguation rules $k=2$. When there is no word in one of the positions contemplated in the context, we adopted the use of an extra tag named 'None'.

5.2 Particles' Evaluation

The quality of a particle is given by the tagging quality of the full input sentence. To evaluate the tagging of the sentence, we use the disambiguated rules to measure the quality of each instance extracted from the sentence. The quality of the overall tagging is given by the sum of the evaluation results for each instance. Let's consider t_i to be the class presented in the last position of the 16-tuple of instance $instance_k$. If R_{t_i} represents the set of disambiguation rules for the lexical category t_i, and $r_k \in R_{t_i}$ a disambiguation rule that covers the instance $instance_k$, then the quality value of $instance_k$ is given by the quality measure Q_k associated with rule r_k.

$$F(instance_k) = \begin{cases} Quality(r_k) & \text{if } r_k \text{ is found} \\ 0 & \text{otherwise} \end{cases} \quad (9)$$

If S_p is the set of all instances extracted from the annotated sentence determined by the particle p, the quality of particle p is given by

$$Fitness(p) = \sum_{i \in S_p} F(i) \quad (10)$$

Although a particle only suggests tags for the ambiguous words in the sentence, the quality of the instances defined by the unambiguous words is affected by the tags established by the particle. Therefore, the overall tagging evaluation should also consider these instances.

6 Experimental Results

We tested our PSO-Tagger on two different languages: English and Portuguese. For the English language we carry out experiments on two different corpora: in a test set of the WSJ corpus of the Penn Treebank made of 8300 tokens, and on a test set of 22562 tokens of the Brown corpus. In both cases the POS-Tagger received as input the set of disambiguation rules learned from the Brown corpus.

For the Portuguese language, we tested the tagger on a test set of the Mac-Morpho corpus with 21466 tokens. In this case the algorithm received as input the set of disambiguation rules learned from the Mac-Morpho training set.

We ran the algorithm 20 times with a swarm of 10 and 20 particles during 50 and 100 generations for the three corpora. The results achieved are shown in table 1. As we can see, the best average accuracy on the WSJ corpus was 96.91% and the best average accuracy on the Brown corpus was 96.72%. The best results on the Brown corpus were achieved with a swarm of 20 particles over 50 generations. A maximum accuracy of 96.75% was found. A swarm of 20 particles over 100 generations gave the best results for the WSJ corpus. In this case, the best tagging found had an accuracy of 97.04%.

For the Portuguese corpus, the best average accuracy obtained was 96.83%, when the POS-tagger was executed with 10 particles over 100 generations. The best accuracy, 96.89%, was found during a run of the algorithm with 20 particles over 50 generations.

Both results allow us to conclude that the PSO-Tagger usually finds a solution very quickly. Like we said before, this algorithm works well with small swarms and tends to converge fast to a solution. Table 2 presents the best results achieved by the approaches we mentioned earlier, along with the best ones achieved by the PSO-Tagger. Observing table 2, we can see that the PSO-Tagger accuracy is very promising, since it is among the best values presented.

Naturally, the difficulty level of the tagging task depends on the number of ambiguous words of the sentence we want to tag. Although it is possible to construct sentences in which every word is ambiguous (Hindle, 1989), such as the following: "Her hand had come to rest on that very book."; those situations are not the most common. After counting the number of ambiguous words that appear in the sentences of the 10% of the Brown corpus we reserved for testing the tagger, we observed that, in average, there are 6.9 ambiguous words per sentence. This

Corpus	Particles	Generations	Average	Standard Deviation	Best
Brown	10	50	96.68	0.022	96.72
		100	96.67	0.028	96.72
	20	50	**96.7**	0.024	**96.75**
		100	96.69	0.024	96.73
WSJ	10	50	96.9	0.054	96.99
		100	**96.91**	0.054	**97.04**
	20	50	96.88	0.053	96.99
		100	96.91	0.031	96.98
Mac-Morpho	10	50	96.82	0.029	96.86
		100	**96.83**	0.029	96.86
	20	50	96.82	0.033	**96.89**
		100	96.81	0.026	96.86

Table 1: Results achieved on the English and Portuguese corpora by the PSO-Tagger after 20 runs with a swarm of size 10 and 20, during 50 and 100 generations.

explain the considerable low number of particles and generations needed to achieve a solution. We could argue that in those conditions the use of a PSO algorithm is unnecessary, and that a exhaustive search could be applied to solve the problem. However, we can not ignore the worst case scenario, where, like we see above, all the words, or a large majority of the words, on a very long sentence may be ambiguous. Furthermore, we observed that the sentence average size of the Brown corpus is of 20.25 tokens, with a maximum of 180. The largest number of ambiguous words on a sentence belonging to this corpus is 68. Even for the smallest degree of ambiguity, with only two possible tags for each word, we have a search space of 2^{68}, which fully justifies the use of a global search algorithm such as a PSO.

The results achieved show that there are no significant differences on the accuracy obtained by the tagger on the two test sets of the English language. At this point, it is important to emphasize that the disambiguation rules used on the tagger were extracted from a subset (different from the test set used in this experiments) of the Brown corpus. Which bring us to the conclusion that the learned rules are generic enough to be used on different corpora, and are not domain dependent. The results achieved for the Portuguese language showed that our strategy also performed well for other languages different from English.

7 Conclusions

We described a new evolutionary approach to the POS tagging problem that achieved competitive results when compared to the best ones published (see table 2). Although there are other approaches to this task based on evolutionary algorithms, in particular genetic algorithms, as far as we know this is the first attempt that uses a PSO algorithm to tackle the POS problem. Our method also differs from previous ones on the information model used to guide the evolutionary process. More specifically, in this work, we used a set of disambiguation rules, including morphological information, in opposition to the stochastic data that is usually adopted in the evolutionary approaches we have found in the literature. We believe that this approach brings a important level of generalization to the model, which results in good tagging performances even when applied to other corpora. Beside the traditional experiments made on English corpora,

Corpus	Tagger	Training Set	Test Set	Average	Best
Brown	PSO-Tagger	50000	22562	96.7	**96.75**
	(Araujo, 2002)	185000	2500	-	95.4
	GA (Alba et al., 2006)	165276	17303	96.37	96.67
	PGA (Alba et al., 2006)	165276	17303	96.61	96.75
WSJ	PSO-Tagger	none	8300	96.91	**97.04**
	(Wilson and Heywood, 2005)	600000	none	-	89.8
	(Brill, 1995)	600000	150000	-	97.2
	(Alba et al., 2006)	554923	2544	-	96.63
Mac-Morpho	PSO-Tagger	107200	21466	96.83	**96.86**
	ETL-Tagger	1M	200K	-	96.75

Table 2: Results achieved by the PSO-Tagger on corpora of English and Portuguese language, along with the results achieved by the approaches more similar to the one presented here. The ETL-Tagger are the one presented in (Nogueira Dos Santos et al., 2008)

we also tested our strategy on a different language, namely the Portuguese language. The results attained showed that the tagger also achieves competitive accuracy when applied to the Portuguese language.

The PSO-Tagger proved to be capable of tackling the combinatorial optimization problem, performing the tagging task with good results, while using limited resources in terms of swarm size and number of generations. Although we consider our results to be promising, we are aware of the necessity of evaluating our approach with a larger tag set and of applying it to more corpora. We also believe that the algorithms' parameters could be better tuned, and for that we intend to conduct a larger set of experiments. Likewise, we think that further experiments, with different sets of attributes for the disambiguation rules, should be conducted. Finally, we think that the overall evolutionary approach could be successfully applied to other disambiguation problems, like the phrase chunking and named-entity recognition problems.

References

Aires, R. V. X., Aluísio, S. M., Kuhn, D. C. e. S., Andreeta, M. L. B., and Oliveira, Jr., O. N. (2000). Combining classifiers to improve part of speech tagging: A case study for brazilian portuguese. In *International Joint Conference, 7th Ibero-American Conference, 15th Brazilian Symposium on AI, IBERAMIA-SBIA 2000, Open Discussion Track Proceedings on AI*, pages 227–236. ICMC/USP.

Alba, E., Luque, G., and Araujo, L. (2006). Natural language tagging with genetic algorithms. *Inf. Process. Lett.*, 100(5):173–182.

Araujo, L. (2002). Part-of-speech tagging with evolutionary algorithms. In Gelbukh, A., editor, *Computational Linguistics and Intelligent Text Processing*, volume 2276 of *Lecture Notes in Computer Science*, pages 187–203. Springer Berlin / Heidelberg.

Araujo, L. (2004). Symbiosis of evolutionary techniques and statistical natural language processing. *Evolutionary Computation, IEEE Transactions on*, 8(1):14 – 27.

Araujo, L. (2007). How evolutionary algorithms are applied to statistical natural language processing. *Artificial Intelligence Review*, 28(4):275–303.

Araujo, L., Luque, G., and Alba, E. (2004). Metaheuristics for natural language tagging. In *Genetic and Evolutionary Computation - GECCO 2004, Genetic and Evolutionary Computation Conference*, volume 3102 of *Lecture Notes in Computer Science*, pages 889–900. Springer.

Brants, T. (2000). Tnt: a statistical part-of-speech tagger. In *Proceedings of the sixth conference on Applied natural language processing*, ANLC '00, pages 224–231, Stroudsburg, PA, USA. Association for Computational Linguistics.

Brill, E. (1995). Transformation-based error-driven learning and natural language processing: a case study in part-of-speech tagging. *Comput. Linguist.*, 21:543–565.

de Jong, K. A., Spears, W. M., and Gordon, D. F. (1993). Using genetic algorithms for concept learning. *Machine Learning*, 13:161–188. 10.1023/A:1022617912649.

Freitas, A. A. (2003). *A survey of evolutionary algorithms for data mining and knowledge discovery*, pages 819–845. Springer-Verlag New York, Inc., New York, NY, USA.

Giordana, A. and Neri, F. (1995). Search-intensive concept induction. *Evol. Comput.*, 3:375–416.

Greene, D. P. and Smith, S. F. (1993). Competition-based induction of decision models from examples. *Machine Learning*, 13:229–257.

Hindle, D. (1989). Acquiring disambiguation rules from text.

Janikow, C. Z. (1993). A knowledge-intensive genetic algorithm for supervised learning. *Machine Learning*, 13:189–228. 10.1007/BF00993043.

Kennedy, J. and Eberhart, R. C. (2001). *Swarm intelligence*. Morgan Kaufmann Publishers Inc., San Francisco, CA, USA.

Kepler, F. and Finger, M. (2006). Comparing two markov methods for part-of-speech tagging of portuguese. In Sichman, J., Coelho, H., and Rezende, S., editors, *Advances in Artificial Intelligence - IBERAMIA-SBIA 2006*, volume 4140 of *Lecture Notes in Computer Science*, pages 482–491. Springer Berlin / Heidelberg. 10.1007/11874850_52.

Noda, E., Freitas, A., and Lopes, H. (1999). Discovering interesting prediction rules with a genetic algorithm. In *Evolutionary Computation, 1999. CEC 99. Proceedings of the 1999 Congress on*, volume 2, pages 3 vol. (xxxvii+2348).

Nogueira Dos Santos, C., Milidiú, R. L., and Rentería, R. P. (2008). Portuguese part-of-speech tagging using entropy guided transformation learning. In *Proceedings of the 8th international conference on Computational Processing of the Portuguese Language*, PROPOR '08, pages 143–152, Berlin, Heidelberg. Springer-Verlag.

Poli, R. (2008). Analysis of the publications on the applications of particle swarm optimisation. *J. Artif. Evol. App.*, 2008:4:1–4:10.

Sousa, T., Silva, A., and Neves, A. (2004). Particle swarm based data mining algorithms for classification tasks. *Parallel Comput.*, 30(5-6):767–783.

Steven Bird, E. K. and Loper, E. (2009). *Natural Language Processing with Python*. O'Reilly Media.

Wilson, G. and Heywood, M. (2005). Use of a genetic algorithm in brill's transformation-based part-of-speech tagger. In *Proceedings of the 2005 conference on Genetic and evolutionary computation*, GECCO '05, pages 2067–2073, New York, NY, USA. ACM.

Optimization for Efficient Determination of Chunk in Automatic Evaluation for Machine Translation

Hiroshi Echizen'ya[1] *Kenji Araki*[2] *Eduard Hovy*[3]
(1) Hokkai-Gakuen University, S 26-Jo, W 11-Chome, Chuo-ku, Sapporo 064-0926 Japan
(2) Hokkaido University, N 14-Jo, W 9-Chome, Kita-ku, Sapporo 060-0814 Japan
(3) Carnegie Mellon University, 5000 Forbes Avenue, Pittsburgh, PA 15213 USA
echi@lst.hokkai-s-u.ac.jp, araki@media.eng.hokudai.ac.jp, hovy@cmu.edu

ABSTRACT
For automatic evaluation of machine translation, translation quality is commonly measuredly counting the number of chunks (consecutive words) that match between reference and candidate texts. For example, METEOR, GTM, ROUGE-W, and IMPACT all use chunks. The length and nature of chunks affects the measured result. IMPACT, a system that can determine the most suitable chunk, requires much processing time because it must scan a regular two-dimensional dynamic programming table. In this paper, we propose a new optimization method to determine chunks efficiently. Moreover, we developed a new automatic evaluation system using lemmas as lexical knowledge. We designate this system as **M**etric Using **L**emma and **O**ptimization for **C**hunk (MLOC). Through evaluation experiments, we confirm that the processing time of MLOC is shorter than that of IMPACT for reference and candidate text pairs with long sentences, although the lexical knowledge is used in MLOC, and MLOC indicates the highest correlation with human judgment among several automatic evaluation systems based on chunks.

KEYWORDS: Automatic evaluation, Chunk, Dynamic programming, Tree structure, Lexical knowledge, Machine translation.

Proceedings of the First International Workshop on Optimization Techniques for Human Language Technology, pages 17–30,
COLING 2012, Mumbai, December 2012.

1 Introduction

In the field of machine translation, various methods for automatic evaluation have been proposed. The ULC(Giménez and Màrquez, 2007), MaxSim(Chan and Ng, 2008), and RTE(Padó et al., 2009) are known to produce high correlations with human judgment. Nevertheless, these methods are not widely used in machine translation because it is difficult to build the systems based on their methods. This problem might be solved when the systems are released on a web site. In contrast, BLEU(Papineni et al., 2002), NIST(NIST, 2002), PER(Su et al., 1992), and WER(Leusch et al., 2003) are used widely because we can build the systems easily based on their methods, and because their processing time is very short. However, these methods produce lower correlations with human judgment. Especially, the correlations assessed at the single-sentence level are quite low.

METEOR(Banerjee and Lavie., 2005), GTM(Turian et al., 2003), ROUGE-W(Lin and Och, 2004), and IMPACT(Echizen-ya and Araki, 2007), which are based on matching chunks between the reference and candidate texts, are effective for sentence-level correlation with human judgment. The chunk is a string of consecutive words considered for matching. The system IMPACT yields the highest correlations among various automatic evaluation methods in sentence-level correlations(Echizen-ya et al., 2009). IMPACT determines the most suitable chunk using information related to chunk length and position. However, IMPACT has a severe problem: it needs much process time to determine suitable chunks. This problem becomes an obstacle to realization of a practical automatic evaluation system using linguistic knowledge, although the quality of the system might improve when linguistic knowledge is used. Therefore, we propose an optimization method to determine the chunk efficiently in automatic evaluation based on chunks.

Our method generates a tree structure based on nodes corresponding to matching words. Consequently, it uses no dynamic programming table that includes information about non-matching words. Moreover, our method approximates the tree structure selecting the nodes which are important to determine suitable chunks. We developed a new automatic evaluation system based on our optimization method and use a lemma as lexical knowledge. We designate this system as **M**etric Using **L**emma and **O**ptimization for **C**hunk (MLOC). Our evaluation experiments indicate that the processing time of MLOC is shorter than that of IMPACT in reference and candidate text pairs containing long sentences, even though MLOC uses lemmas. Therefore, our optimization method is effective to decrease processing time. Moreover, we confirmed that MLOC provided the highest correlation with human judgments among several automatic evaluation systems based on chunks. Therefore, our optimization method is effective to develop a higher-quality and practical automatic evaluation system.

2 Problems of automatic evaluation method based on chunks

In METEOR, GTM, and ROUGE-W, no suitable chunk can be determined because the systems depend only on chunk length. However, IMPACT can determine suitable chunks using information about both chunk length and position. To do so, much processing time is needed.

For example, Table 1 shows a regular two-dimensional dynamic program table computing the Longest Common Subsequence (LCS) for two sequences as follows:

reference: glass guide of the plastic mounting panel P

candidate: a glass guide molded in panel member P made of resin

i		j	1	2	3	4	5	6	7	8	9	10	11	12
		n_j	a	glass	guide	mold -ed	in	panel	mem -ber	P	made	of	the	resin
i	m_i	0	0	0	0	0	0	0	0	0	0	0	0	0
1	glass	0	0	**1**	1	1	1	1	1	1	1	2	2	2
2	guide	0	0	1	**2**	2	2	2	2	2	2	2	2	2
3	of	0	0	1	2	2	2	2	2	2	2	**3**	3	3
4	the	0	0	1	2	2	2	2	2	2	2	3	**4**	4
5	plas -tic	0	0	1	2	2	2	2	2	2	2	3	4	4
6	mount -ing	0	0	1	2	2	2	2	2	2	2	3	4	4
7	panel	0	0	1	2	2	2	**3**	3	3	3	3	4	4
8	P	0	0	1	2	2	2	3	3	**4**	4	4	4	4

Table 1: Example 1: A dynamic programming table.

In Table 1, the values (*i.e.*, i and j) outside of the table respectively denote the word positions in reference and candidate. The word number of the candidate is 12, which is the maximum value of j, and the word number of the reference is 8, which is the maximum value of i. The values in the table are obtained by Eq. (1).

$$D_{i,j} = \begin{cases} 0, & i = 0 \text{ or } j = 0 \\ max(D_{i-1,j}, D_{i,j-1}), & m_i \neq n_j \\ D_{i-1,j-1} + 1, & m_i = n_j \end{cases} \tag{1}$$

The length of LCS is 4 by Eq. (1) in Table 1. Moreover, the number of LCS routes is 2. The LCS routes are the sequences of matching words between the candidate and the reference. In Table 1, two LCS routes are obtained from the candidate and reference as shown below.

LCS route No.1
reference: [glass guide] of the plastic mounting [panel] [P]
candidate: a [glass guide] molded in [panel] member [P] made of the resin
LCS route No.2
reference: [glass guide] [of the] plastic mounting panel P
candidate: a [glass guide] molded in panel member P made [of the] resin

In LCS route No. 1, the matching words are "glass", "guide", "panel", and "P". In LCS route No. 2, the matching words are "glass", "guide", "of", and "the". These matching words correspond to bold values in Table 1. The consecutive matches form the chunk. Therefore, the number of chunks is 3 (*i.e.*, "glass guide", "panel", "P") in LCS route No. 1, and the number of chunks is 2 (*i.e.*, "glass guide", "of the") in LCS route No. 2. In this example, LCS route No. 1 must be selected because it has the most suitable chunk. In LCS route No. 2, "of the" in the candidate does not correspond to "of the" in the reference. Therefore, LCS route No. 1 has a more suitable chunk compared with LCS route No. 2.

In the determination of chunks, ROUGE-W and METEOR select LCS route No. 2, focusing only on chunk length. In LCS route No. 2, the quantities of words in two chunks ("glass guide", "of the") are 2. Moreover, in LCS route No. 1, the quantities of words in three chunks ("glass guide", "panel", "the") are, respectively, 2, 1, and 1. Therefore, METEOR selects LCS route No. 2, for which the number of chunks is small, because the penalty becomes a small value in the calculation of the score, and ROUGE-W also selects LCS route No. 2, for which the lengths of two chunks are 2.

In contrast, IMPACT selects LCS route No. 1 because it uses information of the position of the chunk, not only the chunk length. In LCS route No. 2, the positions of "of the" in candidate and reference are largely different. In IMPACT, the score is calculated using the length and position of chunk in each LCS route when several LCS routes are obtained following Eqs. (2) and (3). Only one LCS route, which has the highest score, is selected.

$$score = \sum_{c \in c\_num} (length(c)^{\beta} \times pos) \quad (2)$$

$$pos = \left(1.0 - |\frac{c_i}{m} - \frac{c_j}{n}|\right) \quad (3)$$

In Eq. (2), c means the chunks, and β is the weight parameter based on the length of each chunk ($\beta > 1.0$). The pos signifies the difference of the relative position of the chunk c between the candidate and reference. In Eq. (3), m and n respectively indicate the quantities of words in the candidate and reference. In addition, c_i and c_j respectively indicate the position of chunks of the candidate and reference. The score in LCS route No. 1 is $3.4933(= 2^{1.2} \times (1.0 - |\frac{1}{8} - \frac{2}{12}|) + 1^{1.2} \times (1.0 - |\frac{7}{8} - \frac{6}{12}|) + 1^{1.2} \times (1.0 - |\frac{8}{8} - \frac{8}{12}|))$ when β is 1.2, and the score in LCS route No. 2 is $3.4461(= 2^{1.2} \times (1.0 - |\frac{1}{8} - \frac{2}{12}|) + 2^{1.2} \times (1.0 - |\frac{3}{8} - \frac{10}{12}|))$. Therefore, IMPACT selects LCS route No. 1, whose score is higher than that of LCS route No. 2. As is clear, it is important for automatic evaluation based on chunks should use information about both the length and position of chunks.

However, IMPACT has a very severe problem. It requires much processing time to search all LCS routes to determine the LCS route which has the most suitable chunks. Moreover, in that case, IMPACT must scan all values of cells in the dynamic programming table although almost all values do not correspond to words that match between the candidate and reference texts. In ROUGE-W and METEOR, not much processing time is needed because they do not consider all LCS routes to determine the chunks. However, they cannot select the most suitable chunks. One way or the other, automatic evaluation systems based on chunks present severe problems. To solve this problem, we propose an optimization method to determine the most suitable chunk efficiently.

3 Optimization method for chunk determination

3.1 Mapping from the dynamic programming table to the tree structure

Table 2 shows an example of the dynamic programming table generated to obtain matching words for the following the candidate and reference fragments:

reference: array rules determine the limits to designing wiring routes
candidate: for arrangement of restriction on the design rule, the wiring route is determined

	j	1	2	3	4	5	6	7	8	9	10	11	12	13
	n_j	ar -range -ment	of	re -stric -tion	on	the	de -sign	rule	,	the	wir -ing	route	is	de -ter -mined
i m_i	0	0	0	0	0	0	0	0	0	0	0	0	0	0
1 array	0	0	0	0	0	0	0	0	0	0	0	0	0	0
2 rules	0	0	0	0	0	0	0	0	0	0	0	0	0	0
3 de -ter -mine	0	0	0	0	0	0	0	0	0	0	0	0	0	0
4 the	0	0	0	0	0	**1**	1	1	1	**1**	1	1	1	1
5 limit	0	0	0	0	0	1	1	1	1	1	1	1	1	1
6 to	0	0	0	0	0	1	1	1	1	1	1	1	1	1
7 de -sign -ing	0	0	0	0	0	1	1	1	1	1	1	1	1	1
8 of	0	0	**1**	1	1	1	1	1	1	1	1	1	1	1
9 the	0	0	1	1	1	**2**	2	2	2	**2**	2	2	2	2
10 wir -ing	0	0	1	1	1	2	2	2	2	3	**3**	3	3	3
11 routes	0	0	1	1	1	2	2	2	2	3	3	3	3	3

Table 2: Example 2: Dynamic programming table.

In IMPACT, LCS routes of three kinds are obtained from the dynamic programming table of Table 2, scanning all values of cells as described below.

LCS route No.1
reference: array rules determine the limit to designing [of] [the wiring] routes
candidate: arrangement [of] restriction on the design rule , [the wiring] route is determined

LCS route No.2
reference: array rules determine [the] limit to designing of [the wiring] routes
candidate: arrangement of restriction on [the] design rule , [the wiring] route is determined

LCS route No.3
reference: array rules determine the limit to designing [of] [the] [wiring] routes
candidate: arrangement [of] restriction on [the] design rule , the [wiring] route is determined

In the example given above, the LCS routes with the most suitable chunks are LCS route No. 1 and No. 2. LCS route No. 2 is selected in IMPACT by the information of the position of chunk "the". However, IMPACT needs much processing time because it must scan all values of cells that do not correspond to the matching words in Table 2.

Our method replaces the information of the matching words in a dynamic programming table with a tree structure. Therefore, our method can emphasize matching words without scanning the values of cells that do not correspond to the matching words in the dynamic programming table. This means that our method can decrease processing time.

First, our method generates the dynamic programming table and extracts only $D_{[i,j]}$ which correspond to the matching words. In Table 2, the values shown in bold typeface correspond to the matching words. Therefore, all $D_{[i,j]}$ of the matching words are $D_{[4,5]}$, $D_{[4,9]}$, $D_{[8,2]}$, $D_{[9,5]}$, $D_{[9,9]}$ and $D_{[10,10]}$. Our method requires no dynamic programming table after extraction of the matching words. Moreover, our method sorts $D_{[i,j]}$ from large to small values. Each $D_{[i,j]}$ corresponds to a node of the tree structure. Figure 1 presents an example of the sort of $D_{[i,j]}$.

value	$D_{[i,j]}$		
3		$D_{[10,10]}$	
2	$D_{[9,9]}$		$D_{[9,5]}$
1	$D_{[8,2]}$	$D_{[4,5]}$	$D_{[4,9]}$

Figure 1: Example of the sorting of $D_{[i,j]}$.

Our method generates a tree structure linking two $D_{[i,j]}$. Figure 2 shows the algorithm for linking between two nodes in a tree structure.

```
Start:
level_num = # of level in value
for(s = level_num; s > 1; s--)
    num_1 = # of D[i,j]^s
    for(t = 1; t > num_1; t++)
        num_2 = # of D[i,j]^(s-1)
        for(u = 1; u > num_2; u++)
            If i in D[i,j]^t > i in D[i,j]^u and i in D[i,j]^t > j in D[i,j]^u
                D[i,j]^t -> D[i,j]^u    # generation of link
End:
```

Figure 2: Algorithm for a link in the tree structure.

In Fig. 2, the value of *level_num* is 3 because the level of values of $D_{[i,j]}$ is 1–3. Moreover, the value of *num_1* is 1 because $D_{[i,j]}$ in the level of value 3 is only $D_{[10,10]}$ and the value of *num_2* is 2 because $D_{[i,j]}$ in level of value 2 is $D_{[9,9]}$ and $D_{[9,5]}$. Our method compares $D_{[10,10]}$ with $D_{[9,9]}$. As a result, the link is generated because $i = 10$ in $D_{[10,10]}$ is larger than $i = 9$ in $D_{[9,9]}$ and $j = 10$ in $D_{[10,10]}$ is larger than $j = 9$ in $D_{[9,9]}$. Therefore, $D_{[10,10]}$ and $D_{[9,9]}$ can be connected as the matching word sequence. In also $D_{[10,10]}$ and $D_{[9,5]}$, the link is generated because $i = 10$ in $D_{[10,10]}$ is larger than $i = 9$ in $D_{[9,5]}$, and $j = 10$ in $D_{[10,10]}$ is larger than $j = 5$ in $D_{[9,5]}$.

Moreover, our method specifically examines the level of values 2 and 1. As a result, for $D_{[9,5]}$ and $D_{[4,5]}$, the link is not generated because $j = 5$ in $D_{[9,5]}$ is not larger than $j = 5$ in $D_{[4,5]}$. In $D_{[9,5]}$ and $D_{[4,9]}$, the link is not generated because $j = 5$ in $D_{[9,5]}$ is not larger than $j = 9$ in $D_{[4,9]}$. Therefore, $D_{[9,5]}$ is not connected with $D_{[4,5]}$ and $D_{[4,9]}$ as the matching word sequence. Finally, the $D_{[4,9]}$ is deleted as the node because it has no link with other nodes. Figure 3 depicts the tree structure using the algorithm presented in Fig. 2. Our method does not require the scanning of those (many) cells that do not correspond to the matching words in the dynamic programming table. Therefore, our method can decrease the processing time.

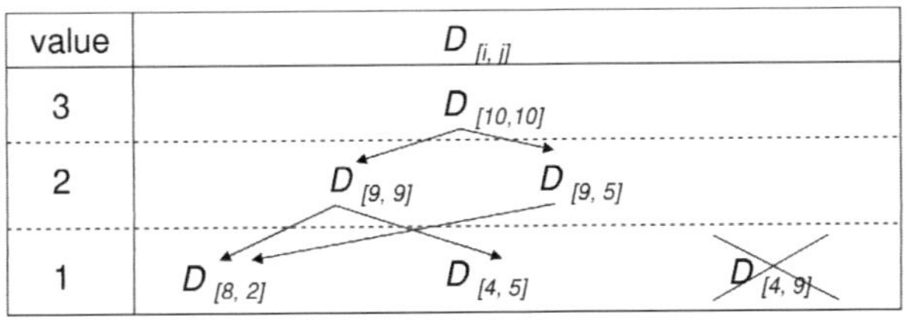

Figure 3: Example of the tree structure.

3.2 Approximation in tree structure

Our method approximates the tree structure using only nodes which are important from the perspective of the length and position of chunks to decrease the processing time. Figure 4 shows the algorithm for selection of nodes in a tree structure.

In our method, the nodes selected are the ones that continue with other nodes, and those for which the difference of relative position between i and j is the smallest among all nodes at one level of value. This means that our method effectively uses both length and position of chunks. In the example of the tree structure in Fig. 3, $D_{[10,10]}$, which is the node at the top level, and $D_{[8,2]}$ and $D_{[4,5]}$, which are the nodes at a lower level, are selected first. Next, our method selects only the most important node among $D_{[9,9]}$ and $D_{[9,5]}$ of level 2.

By Fig. 4, the value of num_1 is 2 (*i.e.*, $D_{[9,9]}$ and $D_{[9,5]}$), and the value of num_2 is 2 (*i.e*, $D_{[8,2]}$ and $D_{[4,5]}$). Therefore, our method compares $D_{[9,9]}$ respectively with $D_{[8,2]}$, $D_{[4,5]}$, and $D_{[9,5]}$ with $D_{[8,2]}$. As a result, neither $D_{[9,9]}$ nor $D_{[9,5]}$ is selected as a node at this time because these nodes are not mutually continuous with $D_{[8,2]}$ and $D_{[4,5]}$. Moreover, the value of num_3 is 1 (*i.e.*, $D_{[10,10]}$). Therefore, our method compares respectively $D_{[9,9]}$ with $D_{[10,10]}$, and $D_{[9,5]}$ with $D_{[10,10]}$. Results show that $D_{[9,9]}$ is selected as a node because $i = 9$ in $D_{[9,9]}$ becomes $i = 10$ in $D_{[10,10]}$ by adding 1 and $j = 9$ in $D_{[9,9]}$ also becomes $j = 10$ in $D_{[10,10]}$ by adding 1: $D_{[9,9]}$ is continuous with $D_{[10,10]}$.

Moreover, our method selects the node for which the difference of word position is the smallest. In this example, the value of differences of word position are, respectively 0.1259 ($=|\frac{9}{11} - \frac{9}{13}|$) in $D_{[9,9]}$ and 0.4336 ($=|\frac{9}{11} - \frac{5}{13}|$) in $D_{[9,5]}$. Therefore, only $D_{[9,9]}$ is selected as the node of tree structure, and $D_{[9,5]}$, which does not continue with other nodes and the difference of word position is not the smallest, is deleted from the tree structure. Figure 5 depicts the final tree structure. Our method obtains the LCS route using only a final tree structure.

```
Start:
        level_num = # of level in value
        for(s = level_num-1; s > 1; s--)
            num_1 = # of D_[i,j]^s
LOOP:       for(t = 1; t > num_1; t++)
                num_2 = # of D_[i,j]^s-1
                for(u = 1; u > num_2; u++)
                    If i in D_[i, j]^t-1== i in D_[i, j]^u and i in D_[i, j]^t-1 == j in D_[i, j]^u
                        tree.node(D_[i, j]^t) # addition node to tree
                        go to LOOP
                num_3 = # of D_[i,j]^s+1
                for(v = 1; v > num_3; v++)
                    If i in D_[i, j]^t+1== i in D_[i, j]^v and i in D_[i, j]^t+1 == j in D_[i, j]^v
                        tree.node(D_[i, j]^t) # addition node to tree
                        go to LOOP
            min_D_[i, j] = min_diff(D_[i,j]^s)
            tree.node(min_D_[i, j]) # addition node to tree
End:
```

Figure 4: Algorithm for selection of nodes in a tree structure.

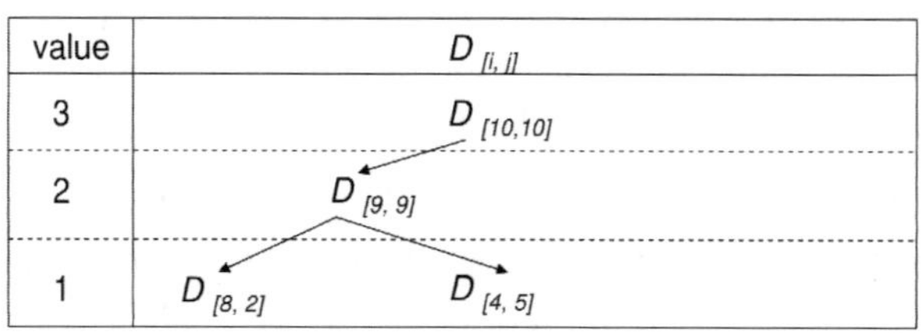

Figure 5: Example of the final tree structure.

As a result, our method can delete LCS routes that have no suitable chunk (*i.e.*, LCS route No. 3 described in Section 3.1): our method can decrease processing time using only necessary $D_{[i,j]}$.

4 MLOC: Automatic evaluation system using lemma

We developed a new automatic evaluation system for machine translation. Our system uses the optimization method described in Section 3. Moreover, it uses a lemma as lexical information to increase the matching words. We designate this system as **M**etric Using **L**emma and **O**ptimization for **C**hunk (MLOC). Consider the following example, using lemmas.

reference: array rule determine the limit to design of the wiring route
candidate: arrangement of restriction on the design rule, the wiring route be determine

MLOC calculates scores using all chunks. To do so, it uses the following Eqs. (4) and (5).

$$R = \left(\frac{\sum_{i=0}^{RN} \left(\alpha^i \sum_{c \in c\_num} length(c)^\beta \right)}{m^\beta} \right)^{\frac{1}{\beta}} \tag{4}$$

$$P = \left(\frac{\sum_{i=0}^{RN} \left(\alpha^i \sum_{c \in c\_num} length(c)^\beta \right)}{n^\beta} \right)^{\frac{1}{\beta}} \tag{5}$$

Eqs. (4) and (5) respectively show the recall and precision. Figure 6 presents an example of determination of all chunks between the reference and candidate.

(1) First process for determination of chunks :
reference :
array rule determine [the] limit to [design] of [the wiring route]
candidate :
arrangement of restriction on [the] [design] rule , [the wiring route] be determine
⇨ i=0: $1^2+1^2+3^2=11$

(2) Second process for determination of chunks :
reference :
array [rule] [determine] [the] limit to [design] of [the wiring route]
candidate :
arrangement of restriction on [the] [design] [rule] , [the wiring route] be [determine]
⇨ i=1: $1^2+1^2=2$

(3) Third process for determination of chunks :
reference :
array [rule] [determine] [the] limit to [design] [of] [the wiring route]
candidate :
arrangement [of] restriction on [the] [design] [rule] , [the wiring route] be [determine]
⇨ i=2: $1^2=1$

Figure 6: Example of determination of all chunks.

MLOC determines only one LCS route using the process described in Section 3. Moreover, LCS routes are determined recursively for all matching words. In Fig. 6, "the", "design", and "the wiring route" are selected as chunks in the first process for determination of chunks. Therefore, the value of $\sum_{c \in c\_num} length(c)^\beta$ is $11(=1^{2.0}+1^{2.0}+3^{2.0})$ when β is 2.0. In the second process for determination of chunks, "rule" and "determine" are selected as chunks. The value of $\sum_{c \in c\_num} length(c)^\beta$ is $2(=1^{2.0}+1^{2.0})$. Finally, "of" is selected as a chunk in the third process for chunk determination. The value of $\sum_{c \in c\_num} length(c)^\beta$ is $1(=1^{2.0})$. Therefore, the value of the Reputation number for determination of suitable LCS (*i.e.*, RN) in Eqs. (4) and (5) becomes 2. The value of $\sum_{i=0}^{RN} \left(\alpha^i \sum_{c \in c\_num} length(c)^\beta \right)$ is $12.25(=0.5^0 \times 11 + 0.5^1 \times 1 + 0.5^2 \times 1)$ when α is 0.5. Moreover, the values of R and P in Eqs. (4) and (5) are, respectively 0.3182 $(=\sqrt{\frac{12.25}{11^{2.0}}})$ and 0.2692 $(=\sqrt{\frac{12.25}{13^{2.0}}})$. MLOC obtains the final score by Eq. (6) as

$$score = \frac{(1+\gamma^2)RP}{R+\gamma^2 P}. \tag{6}$$

In Eq. (6), γ is determined as P/R. The value of γ is 0.8460 when R is 0.2692 and P is 0.3182. The final score is $0.2877 (= \frac{(1+0.8460^2)\times 0.3182\times 0.2692}{0.3182+0.8460^2\times 0.2692})$ by Eq. (6). MLOC can obtain many matching words using lemmas. Moreover, it can obtain the score efficiently determining the suitable LCS route using the optimization process.

5 Experiments

5.1 Experimental Procedure

References and candidates were obtained from patent data in NTCIR-7(Fujii et al., 2008). Using these data, 14 machine translation systems translated 100 Japanese sentences into 100 English sentences. Therefore, the number of candidates is 1,400 ($=14\times 100$). Moreover, four references are given to each candidate obtained by each machine translation system. First, we compared MLOC, our system using only the optimization process (MLOC without lemma) and IMPACT from the perspective of the process time.

Moreover, we calculated the correlation between the scores by the automatic evaluation systems and scores by human judgment. In the scores by human judgment, the human judge evaluated 1,400 candidates from the perspective of adequacy and fluency on a scale of 1 to 5. We used the median value in the evaluation results of three human judges as the final scores of 1–5. We calculated the Pearson's correlation coefficient and Spearman's rank correlation coefficient between the scores obtained using the automatic evaluation systems and the scores by human judgments at the sentence-level and system-level. In the automatic evaluation systems for machine translation, three systems (*i.e.*, MLOC, IMPACT, and ROUGE-W, which are systems based on the chunk) are used. IMPACT especially indicated high correlation coefficients in NTCIR-7 data(Echizen-ya et al., 2009). In ROUGE-W, 1.2 was used as the value of weight parameter for the length of chunk in preliminary experiments. In MLOC and IMPACT, 0.1 was used as the value of penalty parameter (*i.e.*, α) for the difference of chunk sequence and 1.2 was used as the value of weight parameter (*i.e.*, β) for the length of chunks in Eqs. (4) and (5). The MLOC using lemma replaced all words with the lemma in all references and candidates using output obtained by TreeTagger(Schmid, 1994).

5.2 Experimental Results

	all 1,400 pairs	selected 8 pairs
MLOC	202 sec	6 sec
MLOC without lemma	144 sec	5 sec
IMPACT	149 sec	7 sec

Table 3: Processing time.

In Table 3, the processing time of MLOC, MLOC without lemmas, and IMPACT were respectively 202 sec, 144 sec, and 149 sec using all 1,400 pairs of four references and candidates. The processing time of MLOC was the longest because of the use of lemma in creased the number of matches. The processing time of MLOC without lemmas is only 5 sec lower than that of IMPACT. The reason is that the number of LCS routes between the references and candidates are almost invariably small: less than 100. Our optimization method exhibits its strength for cases where the number of LCS routes are large. Therefore, we selected eight pairs of four reference and candidate sentences with more than 300 LCS routes as determined by IMPACT. For this test, IMPACT required 7 sec to process the eight pairs of four references and candidates. However, the processing time was 5 sec for MLOC without lemmas, and 6 sec for MLOC with lemmas. Here, even with the use of lemmas, the processing time of MLOC was shorter than that of IMPACT. These results indicate that our optimization method is effective for decreasing the processing time in the sentences which the number of LCS routes is large.

Table 4 and Table 5 respectively portray Pearson's correlation coefficient in adequacy and fluency. Table 6 and Table 7 respectively portray Spearman's rank correlation coefficient in adequacy and fluency.

	No. 1	No. 2	No. 3	No. 4	No. 5	No. 6	No. 7	No. 8
MLOC	**0.7770**	**0.5405**	**0.4821**	0.5680	0.5477	**0.6310**	**0.6800**	0.7348
MLOC with -out lemma	0.7625	0.5307	0.4704	0.5566	**0.5518**	0.6295	0.6516	**0.7375**
IMPACT	0.7625	0.5307	0.4704	0.5566	**0.5518**	0.6295	0.6516	0.7374
ROUGE-W	0.7648	0.5044	0.4615	**0.5765**	0.5482	0.6257	0.6415	0.7336
	No. 9	No. 10	No. 11	No. 12	No. 13	No. 14	Avg.	System
MLOC	0.7058	0.5691	0.7007	**0.6490**	0.7669	**0.5488**	**0.6358**	0.9271
MLOC with -out lemma	**0.7113**	0.5813	0.7095	0.6251	0.7677	0.5321	0.6298	0.9266
IMPACT	**0.7113**	0.5813	0.7097	0.6251	**0.7685**	0.5321	0.6299	0.9264
ROUGE-W	0.7072	**0.5938**	**0.7131**	0.6099	0.7643	0.5402	0.6275	**0.9400**

Table 4: Pearson's correlation coefficient in adequacy.

	No. 1	No. 2	No. 3	No. 4	No. 5	No. 6	No. 7	No. 8
MLOC	**0.5768**	**0.3880**	**0.3999**	**0.5857**	0.4728	0.5630	**0.5383**	**0.7112**
MLOC with -out lemma	0.5543	0.3765	0.3705	0.5548	**0.4737**	0.5786	0.5168	0.6968
IMPACT	0.5543	0.3765	0.3705	0.5548	**0.4737**	0.5786	0.5168	0.6968
ROUGE-W	0.5566	0.3501	0.3504	0.5715	0.4693	**0.5791**	0.5006	0.6941
	No. 9	No. 10	No. 11	No. 12	No. 13	No. 14	Avg.	System
MLOC	0.5517	0.5243	0.6272	**0.3803**	**0.6129**	0.3897	**0.5223**	0.9382
MLOC with -out lemma	**0.5564**	0.5514	0.6333	0.3727	0.6081	0.4012	0.5175	0.9382
IMPACT	**0.5564**	0.5514	0.6333	0.3728	0.6081	0.4012	0.5175	0.9381
ROUGE-W	0.5480	**0.5520**	**0.6410**	0.3568	0.6003	**0.4078**	0.5127	**0.9426**

Table 5: Pearson's correlation coefficient in fluency.

In Tables 4–7, Nos. 1–14 denote the respective machine translation systems in NTICR-

	No. 1	No. 2	No. 3	No. 4	No. 5	No. 6	No. 7	No. 8
MLOC	**0.7513**	0.4609	**0.5196**	0.5738	**0.4902**	**0.6395**	**0.6530**	**0.6539**
MLOC without lemma	0.7468	**0.4618**	0.4923	0.5666	0.4877	0.6280	0.6196	0.6464
IMPACT	0.7468	**0.4618**	0.4923	0.5666	0.4877	0.6280	0.6196	0.6460
ROUGE-W	0.7379	0.4494	0.4943	**0.5786**	0.4785	0.6166	0.5902	0.6375
	No. 9	No. 10	No. 11	No. 12	No. 13	No. 14	Avg.	System
MLOC	**0.6882**	0.5510	0.6982	**0.6195**	0.7439	**0.5864**	**0.6164**	0.9824
MLOC without lemma	0.6859	0.5478	0.7171	0.5960	0.7433	0.5836	0.6088	**0.9912**
IMPACT	0.6859	0.5478	0.7171	0.5971	0.7442	0.5836	0.6089	**0.9912**
ROUGE-W	0.6734	**0.5653**	**0.7195**	0.5737	**0.7448**	0.5682	0.6020	**0.9912**

Table 6: Spearman's rank correlation coefficient in adequacy.

	No. 1	No. 2	No. 3	No. 4	No. 5	No. 6	No. 7	No. 8
MLOC	**0.5715**	**0.3732**	**0.3799**	**0.5829**	0.4101	**0.6169**	**0.4880**	**0.6590**
MLOC without lemma	0.5520	0.3518	0.3643	0.5488	**0.4119**	0.5995	0.4691	0.6321
IMPACT	0.5520	0.3518	0.3643	0.5488	**0.4119**	0.5995	0.4691	0.6325
ROUGE-W	0.5426	0.3359	0.3472	0.5482	0.4066	0.5898	0.4497	0.6275
	No. 9	No. 10	No. 11	No. 12	No. 13	No. 14	Avg.	System
MLOC	0.5436	0.4339	0.6469	**0.3689**	0.6363	0.4117	**0.5089**	0.9165
MLOC without lemma	**0.5452**	0.4661	0.6548	0.3590	**0.6371**	**0.4437**	0.5025	**0.9253**
IMPACT	**0.5452**	0.4661	0.6544	0.3586	0.6359	**0.4437**	0.5024	**0.9253**
ROUGE-W	0.5277	**0.4738**	**0.6686**	0.3423	0.6283	0.4241	0.4937	**0.9253**

Table 7: Spearman's rank correlation coefficient in fluency.

7. Their values are correlation coefficients at the sentence level. In the tables, "Avg." signifies the average values of 14 correlation coefficients. "System" stands for the correlation coefficients at the system level. Bold values show the highest correlation coefficient among four automatic evaluation systems.

5.3 Discussion

We describe the influence of the optimization method from the perspective of the scores. In Tables 4–7, the difference between MLOC without lemmas and IMPACT depends on whether the optimization method described in Section 3 is used or not. Therefore, in MLOC without lemmas and IMPACT of Tables 4–7, we can confirm the influence of the optimization method on scores. Results show that the influence of the optimization method is very slight because the difference of values for the correlation coefficient of "Avg." and "System" between MLOC without lemmas and IMPACT is 0.0001 or 0.0002 in Tables 4–7. The scores of MLOC without lemmas are almost identical to the scores of IMPACT. Therefore, we confirm that the influence of the optimization method is very slight on scores.

In the correlation coefficient, MLOC indicated the highest values among four systems. Table 8 presents the average values of "Avg." and "System" in Tables 4–7. In Table 8, the total average value of correlation coefficient of MLOC is the highest among four systems. The reason is that MLOC is extremely effective at the sentence level. The numbers for which MLOC obtained the highest correlation coefficient among four systems in 14 machine translation systems (*i.e.*, the quantities of bold values in MLOC) are, respectively, 7, 8, 9, and 8 in Tables 4, 5, 6 and 7. These results show that MLOC is extremely effective for sentence-level evaluation.

	Pearson in adequacy	Pearson in fluency	Spearman in adequacy	Spearman in fluency	Avg.
MLOC	0.7815	0.7303	0.7994	0.7127	**0.7560**
MLOC with -out lemma	0.7782	0.7279	0.8000	0.7139	0.7550
IMPACT	0.7781	0.7278	0.8001	0.7138	0.7550
ROUGE-W	0.7838	0.7277	0.7966	0.7095	0.7544

Table 8: Average values of "Avg." and "System".

6 Conclusion

In this paper we propose an optimization method for the efficient determination of chunks for automatic evaluation of machine translation output using chunk-based matching, and developed MLOC as a new automatic evaluation system. The experimentally obtained results demonstrate that the processing time of MLOC is shorter than that of IMPACT for the pairs of reference and candidate fragments in which the number of LCS route is more than 300, even though lemmas are used in MLOC. These results indicate that our optimization method is effective to decrease the processing time.

Moreover, we performed experiments to confirm the quality of MLOC from the perspective of the automatic evaluation system. Our evaluation experiments confirm that MLOC can obtain the highest correlation coefficients among other systems based on chunks. This means that our optimization method is effective to realize higher quality automatic evaluation for machine translation.

Future studies will use a part-of-speech as effective lexical knowledge to improve MLOC quality. Moreover, we plan to use MLOC for parameter tuning in SMT.

Acknowledgments

This work was done as research under the AAMT/JAPIO Special Interest Group on Patent Translation. The Japan Patent Information Organization (JAPIO) and the National Institute of Information (NII) provided corpora used in this work. The author gratefully acknowledges support from JAPIO and NII. Also, this work was partially supported by Grants from the High-Tech Research Center of Hokkai-Gakuen University.

References

Jesús Giménez and Lluís Màrquez. (2007). Heterogeneous Automatic MT Evaluation Through Non-Parametric Metric Combinations, *In Proceedings of the IJCNLP'07,* pp.319–326.

Yee Seng Chan and Hwee Tou Ng. (2008). MAXSIM: An Automatic Metric for Machine Translation Evaluation Based on Maximum Similarity, *In Proceedings of the MetricMATR Workshop of AMTA-2008*, pp.319–326.

Sebastian Padó, Michel Galley, Dan Jurafsky and Christopher D. Manning. (2009). Textual Entailment Features for Machine Translation Evaluation, *In Proceedings of the Fourth Workshop on Statistical Machine Translation*

Kishore Papineni, Salim Roukos, Todd Ward and Wei-Jing Zhu. 2002. BLEU: a Method for Automatic Evaluation of Machine Translation. *In Proc. of ACL'02*, pp.311–318.

NIST. 2002. Automatic Evaluation of Machine Translation Quality Using N-gram Co-Occurrence Statistics. *http://www.nist.gov/speech/tests/mt/doc/ngram-study.pdf.*

Keh-Yih Su, Ming-Wen Wu and Jing-Shin Chang. 1992. A New Quantitative Quality Measure for Machine Translation Systems. *In Proc. of GOLING'92*, pp.433–439.

Gregor Leusch, Nicola Ueffing and Hermann Ney. 2003. A Novel String-to-String Distance Measure with Applications to Machine Translation Evaluation. *In Proc. of MT Summit IX*, pp.240–247.

Satanjeev Banerjee and Alon Lavie. 2005. METEOR: An Automatic Metric for MT Evaluation with Improved Correlation with Human Judgments. *In Proc. of ACL Workshop on Intrinsic and Extrinsic Evaluation Measures for Machine Translation and/or Summarization*, pp.65–72.

Joseph P. Turian, Luke Shen and I. Dan Melamed. 2003. Evaluation of Machine Translation and its Evaluation. *In Proc. of MT Summit IX*, pp.386–393.

Chin-Yew Lin and Franz Josef Och. (2004). Automatic Evaluation of Machine Translation Quality Using Longest Common Subsequence and Skip-Bigram Statistics, *In Proceedings of the ACL'04*, pp.606–613.

Hiroshi Echizen-ya and Kenji Araki. 2007. Automatic Evaluation of Machine Translation based on Recursive Acquisition of an Intuitive Common Parts Continuum. *In Proc. of MT Summit XII*, pp.151–158.

Hiroshi Echizen-ya, Terumasa Ehara, Sayori Shimohata, Atsushi Fujii, Masao Utiyama, Mikio Yamamoto, Takehito Utsuro and Noriko Kando. 2009. Meta-Evaluation of Automatic Evaluation Methods for Machine Translation using Patent Translation Data in NTCIR-7. *In Proc. of the Third Workshop on Patent Translation*, pp.9–16.

Atsushi Fujii, Masao Utiyama, Mikio Yamamoto and Takehito Utsuro. 2008. Overview of the Patent Translation Task at the NTCIR-7 Workshop. *In Proc. of Seventh NTCIR Workshop Meeting on Evaluation of Information Access Technologies: Information Retrieval, Question Answering and Cross-lingual Information Access*, pp.389–400.

Helmut Schmid. 1994. Probabilistic Part-of-Speech Tagging Using Decision Trees. *In Proc. of International Conference on New Methods in Language Processing* pp.389–400.

Optimizing Transliteration for Hindi/Marathi to English Using only Two Weights

M L Dhore[1] *S K Dixit*[2] *R M Dhore*[3]
(1)LINGUISTIC RESEARCH GROUP, VIT, Pune, Maharashtra, India
(2) LINGUISTIC RESEARCH GROUP, WIT, Solapur, Maharashtra, India
(3) LINGUISTIC RESEARCH GROUP, PVG COET, Pune, Maharashtra, India
manikrao.dhore@vit.edu,headextcwitsolapur@gmail.com,ruchidhore93@gmail.com

ABSTRACT

Machine transliteration has received significant research attention in last two decades. It is observed that Hindi to English and Marathi to English named entity machine transliteration is comparably less studied. Currently, research work in this domain is carried out by using grapheme based statistical approaches. But, to achieve better accuracy for the transliteration, an adequate bilingual text corpus is a mandatory requirement for statistical approaches.

This paper focuses on Hindi to English and Marathi to English direct machine transliteration of Indian-origin named entities such as proper names, place names and organization names. Proposed phonetic based statistical approach uses phoneme and named entity length as features for supervised learning and transliterates them in English using full consonant based phonetic scheme without support of corpus. This system takes Indian origin named entities as an input in Hindi and Marathi using Devanagari script and transliterates it into English by using only two weights.

KEYWORDS: Machine Transliteration, Named Entity, Full Consonant, Supervised Learning.

Proceedings of the First International Workshop on Optimization Techniques for Human Language Technology, pages 31–48,
COLING 2012, Mumbai, December 2012.

1. Introduction

Historically, India has been a multilingual country and Indian constitution officially recognizes 22 languages with 11 different scripts and 6000 dialects used in different states spread across the country (Mudur 1999). Hindi is the national language of the India and spoken by more than 500 million Indians. Hindi is the world's fourth most commonly used language after Chinese, English and Spanish. Marathi is one of the widely spoken languages in India especially in the state of Maharashtra. Hindi and Marathi uses the "Devanagari" script for writing and draw their vocabulary mainly from Sanskrit. It is challenging to transliterate out of vocabulary (OOV) words like names and technical terms occurring in the user input across languages with different alphabets and sound inventories. Transliteration is the conversion of a word from one language to another without losing its phonological characteristics. Machine transliteration is usually used to support the machine translation (MT) and cross-language information retrieval (CLIR) to convert the named entities (Padariya 2008).

Existing approaches for Named Entity (hence forth denoted as NE) machine transliterations are linguistic-based and statistical-based (Karimi 2011). The linguistic approach uses hand-crafted rules, based on pattern matching which need a linguistic analysis to formulate rules. Statistical approach tries to generate transliterations using statistical methods based on bilingual text corpora. Transliterations are generated on the basis of statistical models, which are derived from the analysis of bilingual text corpora.

Hindi/Marathi to English direct NE machine transliteration is quite difficult due to the many factors such as difference in writing script, difference in number of characters/alphabets, concept of capitalization of leading characters, phonetic characteristics, relative character length, presence of a number of exonyms, endonyms and historical variants for many place names, number of valid transliterations and availability of the parallel corpus (Saha 2008).

In most of the grapheme based statistical methods parallel corpus is used and trained for the adequate number of entries using one of the learning approaches such as HMM, CRF, SVM etc. As shown below, for the NE / विजयराघवगढ़ (vijayrāghavgarh)/ which is place name, character alignment is obtained using the available tools (like Moses, GIZA++, SRILM,) and then, aligned corpus is trained using one or more statistical probability approaches.

Source Language	Target Language
वि ज य रा घ व ग ढ़	vi ja y rā gha v ga rh

The accuracy of statistical methods depends on how good corpus is prepared and how good learning algorithm is. We have not found any complete named entity bilingual corpus for the Indian languages.

2. Pure and Full Consonant

The basic consonant shape in the Indian script always has the implicit vowel /अ(a)/ and hence there is no explicit matra form for the short vowel 'a'. For example, the NE name /कमल (kamal)/ is linguistically written as कमल = क्+अ+म्+अ+ल्+अ = k+a+m+a+l+a.

However, there are equivalent matras for all the other vowels (ा –ā/A/aa, ि-i, ी-I, ु-u, ू-U, े-e, ै-ai, ो-o, ौ-au), which get attached to the basic consonant shape whenever the corresponding vowel immediately follows the consonant. The written form of a basic consonant without the implicit 'a' vowel either has an explicit shape or it has the graphical sign '्', known as the Halant (or Virama in Marathi) attached to its basic consonant shape (e.g. क्). This is referred to as the 'Halant form' of the consonant or *pure consonant.* The Halant is the vowel अ (a) omission sign. It serves to cancel the inherent vowel अ of the consonant to which it is applied (Mudur 1999).

When Devanagari vowel phoneme 'a' is added to any generic consonant phoneme then the consonant phoneme is called *full consonant.* It is necessary to have inherent 'a' attached to consonant to add the phone of 'a' vowel to it. If inherent 'a' is not added to the independent consonant phoneme, it becomes very difficult to utter its transliteration in English as well as to obtain its back transliteration in Devanagari from English. For example NE /कमल (kəməl)/ will be spelled as /kml/ and would be back transliterated as / क्म्ल/ which is tri-conjunct (Joshi 2003).

Unicode and ISCII character encoding standards for Indic scripts are based on full form of consonants (Singh 2006). Table 1 shows the pure consonants and full consonants with their English equivalent.

Pure Consonant in Devanagari	English Equivalent	Full Consonant in Devanagari	English Equivalent
क्	k	क् + अ = क	ka
ख्	kh	ख् +अ =ख	kha
ग्	g	ग् + अ = ग	ga

TABLE 1 - Pure and Full Consonant

Following are few examples about how to use the pure and full consonant approach.

Pure Consonant Approach

स् + अ + ई = सई (s + a + i = sai)

प् + अ + क् +ई = पकी (p + a + k +i = paki)

Full Consonant Approach

स + ई = सई (sa + i = sai)

प + क + ी = पकी (pa + ka + i)

In proposed approach, the input NE for example / विजयराघवगढ़ /, is segmented into basic syllabic units such as वि ज य रा घ व ग ढ़ and transliterated into English by mapping source language phonetic units into target language phonetic unit using full consonant based phonetic mapping scheme. IAST (International Alphabet of Sanskrit Transliteration) converter can be used to obtain the baseline transliteration. The baseline transliteration for NE / विजयराघवगढ़ / is shown below.

Source Language	Baseline Transliteration
वि ज य रा घ व ग ढ़	vi ja ya rā gha va ga rh

The NE /विजयराघवगड/ is made up of three NEs विजय (Vijay), राघव (Rāghav) and गड (garh) respectively. As it is a multi word NE and consists of three segments, there are three breakpoints (less stressed positions) at /ya/, /va/ and /rh/, hence the inherent 'a' mapped by full consonant mapping should be deleted to get the correct transliteration as /vijayrāghavgarh/.

It is challenging task to find out the number of segments in the given NE, in order to find the boundaries of the segments to remove the inherent 'a' attached due to full consonant mapping. The segments in the NE are obtained by assigning two weights based on the number of diacritics used to form a phonetic unit and the length of the source language NE is used as a feature for supervised learning to obtain the multiple classes for the segmentation. Segmentation is used to identify and delete the schwa (less stressed positions) which is a major issue in direct translation without training the corpus.

3. Related Work

Existing basic models for NE machine transliterations are Grapheme-based and Phoneme-based. The grapheme based model treats transliteration as an orthographic process and tries to map the source language graphemes directly to the target language graphemes. Phoneme-based model considers transliteration as a phonetic process. Under such frameworks, transliteration is treated as a conversion from source grapheme to source phoneme followed by a conversion from source phoneme to target grapheme.

The major contributors in the area of machine transliteration in India are C-DAC (Center for Development of Advanced Computing), NCST (National Center for Software Technology) and Indictrans Team. In the early 1980's, the development of GIST (Graphics and Intelligence - Based Script Technology) was a major breakthrough. C-DAC developed the hardware based solution GIST based on ISCII (Indian Script Code For Information Interchange). The second development was Unicode based encoding standard UTF-8 for Indic script (BIS 1991). The third development (2003) was a phonemic code based scheme for effective processing of Indian languages and used successfully in turnkey jobs such as telephone directory in Hindi, bilingual certificate for Mumbai University, and collector voters' list (Joshi 2003). The applications they have localised are Indian Railways Reservation Charts, Mahanagar Telephone Nigams and Bilingual Telephone Directories.

One of the early works on transliteration is done by Arbabi. They combined neural networks and expert systems for Arabic-English pair using phoneme model (Arbabi 1994). Knight and Graehl developed a five stage statistical model to do back transliteration, that is, to recover the original English name from its transliteration into Japanese Katakana (Knight 1997). Stalls used this for back transliteration from Arabic to English (Stalls 1998). Al-Onaizan and Knight have produced a simpler Arabic-English transliterator and evaluated how well their system can match a source spelling (Al-Onaizan 2002). Their work includes an evaluation of the transliterations in terms of their reasonableness according to human judges. Work in the field of Indian Language CLIR was done by Jaleel and Larkey, which was based on their work in English-Arabic transliteration for CLIR [Jaleel 2003]. Their approach was based on Hidden Markov Model using GIZA++. Phoneme-based models, based on weighted finite state transducers (Knight 1997) and Markov window (Jung 2003) considers transliteration as a phonetic process. OM transliteration scheme provided a script representation which is common for all Indian languages (Ganapathiraju 2005). Punjabi machine transliteration for Punjabi language from Shahmukhi to Gurmukhi used the set of transliteration rules (Malik 2006). Sproat presented a formal computational analysis of Brahmi scripts (Sproat 2002-2004). Kopytonenko focused on computational models that perform grapheme-to-phoneme conversion (Kopytonenko 2006). Ganesh, Harsha, Pingali and

Verma have developed a statistical transliteration technique which is language independent. They selected a statistical model for transliteration which is based on Hidden Markov Model alignment and Conditional Random Fields (Ganesh 2008). Sujan Kumar Saha, Partha Sarathi Ghosh, Sudeshna Sarkar, and Pabitra Mitra have proposed a two-phase transliteration methodology (Saha 2008). The transliteration module uses an intermediate alphabet, which is designed by preserving the phonetic properties. Ekbal, Naskar and Bandyopadhyay made significant attempt to develop transliteration systems for Indian languages to English and especially for Bengali-English transliteration (Ekbal 2007-2010). Manoj K. Chinnakotla, Om P. Damani, and Avijit Satoskar have developed a reasonable transliteration system for resource scared languages by judiciously applying statistical techniques to monolingual resources in conjunction with manually created bilingual rule bases (Chinnakotla 2010). The statistical technique used is the Character Sequence Modeling (CSM), called Language Modelling. They have proved that if the word origin is used for the transliteration, then the system performs better than statistical methods. Jong-Hoon Oh approach is based on two transliteration models (Oh 2009). They used three different machine learning algorithms CRF, MIRA and MEM for building multiple machine transliteration engines. Literature survey shows that the maximum word accuracy achieved is 95.5%, for English to Russian (Martin 2009) using grapheme based statistical approach. In India the maximum word accuracy achieved is 91.59% for Hindi to English (Saha 2008) using phonetic model

4. Approach

The objective of the work is to transliterate named entities from Hindi and Marathi into English. Following Hindi/Marathi language related terminologies are used.

Akshara - It is the minimal articulatory unit of speech in Hindi/Marathi (Pandey 1990).

Swara – It is a pure vowel in Devanagari. Swaras is plural of Swara.

Vyanjana – It is a consonant in Devanagari. Vyanjanas is the plural form of it.

Jodaakshar – It is the conjugates in Devanagari.

Syllable - It is made up of phonetic units to establish minimum rhythm.

Schwa - The schwa is the vowel sound in many lightly pronounced unaccented syllables in words of more than one syllable. It is represented by /ə/ symbol (Naim 2009).

The overall process is carried out as follows.

Step 1: Preparation of phonetic map table for Devanagari to English transliteration using full consonant approach with local language context.

Step 2: Formation of Devanagari Phonetic Units.

Step 3: Generation of Intermediate Phonetic Code (denoted hence forth by IPC) by mapping Devanagari phonetic units to equivalent phonetic unit using phonetic map.

Step 4: Pruning of inherent 'a' generated by vowel matras due to full consonant approach as well as half consonants 'a`' generated by conjuncts (Jodakshar) from intermediate code. (Outcome of this step is denoted hence forth as Modified Intermediate Phonetic Code MIPC).

Step 5: Empirical analysis for multiword named entity formation in Hindi and Marathi.

Step 6: Statistical Model.

Step 7: Segmentation and classification using supervised learning

Step 8: Transliteration Example

4.1 Preparation of phonetic map table

The possibility of different scripts between the source and target languages is the problem that transliteration systems need to tackle. Hindi/Marathi uses the Devanagari script whereas English uses the Roman script. Devanagari script used for Hindi have 12 pure vowels, two additional loan vowels taken from the Sanskrit and one loan vowel from English. According to Cambridge Advanced Learner's Dictionary English has only five pure vowels but, the vowel sound is also associated with the consonants w and y (Koul 2008). There are 34 pure consonants, 5 traditional conjuncts, 7 loan consonants and 2 traditional signs in Devanagari script and each consonant have 14 variations through integration of 14 vowels while in Roman script there are only 21 consonants. The 34 pure consonants and 5 traditional conjuncts along with 14 vowels produce 546 different alphabetical characters (Mudur 1999). Table 2 show 15 vowels along with their matra signs and 34 pure consonants in Devanagari script. The consonant /ळ/ is used only in Marathi language.

Vowel	Matra	Vowel	Matra	Pure consonants				
अ	No matra	ॠ	◌ॄ	क	ख	ग	घ	ङ
आ	◌ा	ए	◌े	च	छ	ज	झ	ञ
इ	◌ि	ऐ	◌ै	ट	ठ	ड	ढ	ण
ई	◌ी	ओ	◌ो	त	थ	द	ध	न
उ	◌ु	औ	◌ौ	प	फ	ब	भ	म
ऊ	◌ू	अं	◌ं	य	र	ल	व	श
ऋ	◌ृ	अः	◌ः	ष	स	ळ	ह	
Loan Vowel		ऑ	◌ॅ					

TABLE 2 - Vowels and Consonant in Hindi and Marathi

Table 3 shows the 5 traditional conjuncts, 7 loan alphabets, 2 traditional signs and 2 special nasal signs in Devanagari script (Walambe 1990].

Traditional Conjuncts	क्ष त्र ज्ञ श्र द्य
Additional Consonants	ड़ ढ़
Loan Consonants	क़ ख़ ग़ ज़ फ़
Traditional Signs	ॐ श्री
Special nasal	◌ं ◌ँ

TABLE 3 - Traditional Conjuncts in Hindi and Marathi

Table 4 shows the phonetic based mapping scheme used to transliterate Devanagari consonant and vowel phones into equivalent English Phones using full consonant approach. It includes all alphabets of Devanagari script used in both Hindi/Marathi and fully based on the National Library of Kolkata and ITRANS of IIT Madras, India (Unicode 2007). It is to note that the first vowel /अ/ in Hindi/Marathi is mapped to English letter 'a' (short vowel) while the second vowel /आ/ is mapped to 'ā' (long vowel as per IPA) in English. The alphabet 'a' in English is a short vowel equivalent to /अ/ which is also a short vowel in Devanagari while /आ/ in Devanagari is a long vowel and mapped capital 'ā' or 'A' in our phonetic scheme to generate the IPC.

व्यंजनवर्ण CONSONANT PHONEME			Glo-ttal	कोमल तालव्य Velar	कठिन तालव्य Palatal	मूर्धन्य Retroflex	दन्त्य Dental	ओष्ठय Labial
स्पर्श Stops	अघोष Voiceless	अल्पप्राण Unaspirated		क क़ ka qa	च cha	ट Ta	त ta	प pa
		महाप्राण Aspirated		ख ख़ kha, khha	छ Cha	ठ Tha	थ tha	फ फ़ pha fa
	सघोष Voiced	अल्पप्राण Unaspirated		ग ग़ ga, ghha	ज ज़ ja za	ड ड़ Da Dha	द da	ब ba
		महाप्राण Aspirated		घ gha	झ jha	ढ ढ़ Dha , rha	ध dha	भ bha
नासिक्य Nasals				ङ nga	ञ nya	ण Na	न na	म ma
Anuswara and Anunasik				M (default)	ं or ँ	N (depends on next consonant)		ं or ँ
अर्धस्वर वर्ण Semivowels					य ya	र ra	ल la	व va/wa
संघर्षी Fractives	अघोष Voiceless		: -h		श sha	ष Sha	स sa	
	सघोष Voiced		ह ha	जिव्हामूलीय विसर्जनीय				उपध्मानीय
स्वरवर्ण VOWEL PHONEMES	ह्रस्व Short		अ a		इ i	ऋ Ru	ऌ lRu	उ u
	दीर्घ Long		आ A/ ā		ई ए I/ee e	ॠ RU	ॡ lRU	ऊ ओ U oo
संयुक्त Diapthongs					ऐ ai			औ au/ou
पारंपारिक जोडाक्षरे Traditional Conjuncts			क्ष ksha	ज्ञ dnya	द्य dya	श्र shra	त्र tra	ॐ om श्री Shree
स्वतंत्र वर्ण Independent Consonant								ळ La

TABLE 4 - Full Consonant based Phonetic Scheme

4.2 Formation of Devanagari Phonetic Units

As Unicode uses full consonant approach it treats Devanagari consonant phoneme and vowel phoneme as a separate units as shown below.

विजयराघवगढ़(Vijayrāghavgarh) -> व + ि + ज + य + र + ा + घ + व + ग +ढ़

This feature of Unicode is very useful in the creation of Devanagari Phonetic Units. From internal representation of Unicode, phonetic units are formed for Devanagari names as shown below.

विजयराघवगढ़ -> वि | ज | य | रा | घ | व | ग | ढ़

4.3 Generation of Intermediate Phonetic Code

The phonetic scheme is based on full consonant approach and dependent on vowel matra 'अ'. The inherent 'a' is added even if any other vowel matra is present with Devanagari phoneme unit. The script generated in English for Devanagari phonetic unit with inherent 'a' using the phonetic mapping scheme is denoted as Intermediate Phonetic Code (IPC). Table 5 shows how IPC in English is generated for the Devanagari consonant phoneme 'क' when it is combined with different vowel phoneme of Devanagari script.

Devanagari Consonant	Devanagari Vowel	Devanagari Vowel Matra	Devanagari Syllabic Unit	IPC in English
क	अ	No Matra	क	ka
क	आ	ा	का	kaA
क	इ	ि	कि	kai
क	ई	ी	की	kaI
क	उ	ु	कु	kau
क	ऊ	ू	कू	kaU
क	ऋ	ृ	कृ	kaRu

TABLE 5 -IPC for Devanagari Consonant 'क'

The following method is used to generate the IPC in English.

- Devanagari name divided into the syllabic units are called as Source Transliteration Units (STU). STU is equivalent to phonetic unit of Devanagari. The STU can be represented using following regular expression.
  STU = ((V) | (C) | (CV) | (CCV) | (C...CV)) (G)
  where C = Consonant, V = Vowel and G = Nasalization of vowels
- English name divided into the syllabic units called as Target Transliteration Units (TTU). TTU is equivalent to a phonetic unit of English. The regular expression for English can be written as TTU = C*V*
- The Devanagari name is represented as a collection of Devanagari phonetic units.
  Name in Devanagari = { STU_1, STU_2, ... STU_n }
- The English name is represented as a collection of English phonetic units.
  Name in English = { TTU_1, TTU_2, ... TTU_m }
- IPC is obtained by using direct mapping of STUs to TTUs on one to one basis.

Table 6 shows the few examples for IPC in English for the Devanagari NE.

NE	STUs	TTUs	IPC in English
नोवरोझाबाद	नो|व|रो|झा|बा|द	nao|va|rao|jhaā|baā|da	naovaraojhaābaāda

TABLE 6 - IPC Examples

4.4 Pruning

An IPC is generated by mapping STUs to TTUs. STUs are generated from the Devanagari name which uses Unicode encoding. Due to the full consonant nature of Unicode, there is an inherent 'a' followed by consonant phoneme for all Devanagari vowel matras in IPC form. The inherent 'a' generated for Devanagari phonetic units having any vowel matra should be removed. One of the problems in Devanagari to English transliteration is the transformation of conjugates. When the half consonant cluster (Virama/Halant ्) appears in Devanagari script, it is mapped in English with the letter symbol 'a`' which appears in between two consonant phonemes. There is no practice to represent such half consonant in English. All the viramas in Devanagari script mapped as a half consonants 'a`' should be eliminated from the IPC. The output after pruning inherent 'a' and 'a`' is denoted as Modified IPC (MIPC). Table 7 shows the example of removal of inherent 'a' if matra or half consonant is present.

STU	TTU	If matra , remove 'a'	If conjunct, remove 'a`	Modified IPC
कै	kaai	kai	---	kailāshanātha
ला	laā	lā	---	
श	sha	---	---	
ना	naā	nā	---	
थ	tha	----	---	

TABLE 7 - IPC to MIPC for Devanagari NE 'Kailashnath'

4.5 Empirical analysis for multiword named entity formation

An example shown in Table -7, the NE /*कैलाशनाथ*/ is transliterated as /*kailāshanātha*/. The NE /*कैलाशनाथ*/ is multi-word name consists of /*कैलाश*/ and a suffix /*नाथ*/ . An 'a' followed by 'sh' should be deleted as well as the last 'a' also should be deleted to obtain the correct transliteration.

कैलाशनाथ → [कै | ला | श | ना | थ] → [kaai | laā| sha | naā | tha] → [kai | lā | sha | nā | tha] → [kai | lā| sh | nā | th] →[kailāsh | nāth] →kailāshnāth

It has been observed that the minimum length of the NE is 1 akshara (formed using 1 syllabic unit) and maximum length is 8 aksharas. There are very few named entities consisting one syllable. From the number of aksharas in the named entities, 8 categories are made. One akshara is considered equivalent to one phonetic unit in the Devanagari NEs. It is found that nearly 50% NEs used in India are a combination of two or more individual named entities (denoted hence forth NEs). For one akshara, two aksharas and three aksharas NEs, transliteration is quite simple. As the length of a NE increases, the segmentation becomes important to find out the number of words used to form the NE in order to separate the rhythms within it and in turn number of phonetic units in each rhythm.

Most of the four aksharas, five aksharas, six aksharas, seven aksharas and eight aksharas NEs are formed with the combination of two or three different rhythmic units. Table 8 shows the observations of possible combinations of phonetic segments from pronunciation point of view.

NE	Segmentation	Segment Lengths
Number of Aksharas =4		
श्रीवर्धन(Shriwardhan)	श्री + वर्धन(Shrī + wardhan)	1 + 3
बाजीराव(Bājīrāo)	बाजी + राव (Bājī+ rāo)	2 + 2
धवलश्री(Dhawalshrī)	धवल + श्री (Dhawal + shrī)	3 + 1
Number of Aksharas =5		
मनमोहन(Manmohan)	मन + मोहन (Man + mohan)	2 + 3
माणिकराव(Mānikrāo)	माणिक + राव (Mānik + rāo)	3 + 2
श्रीनारायण(Shrinārāyan)	श्री + नारायण (Shrī + nārāyan)	1 + 4
Number of Aksharas =6		
करमरकर(Karmarkar)	कर+मर+ कर (Kar + mar + kar)	2 + 2 + 2
प्रेमनारायण(Premnārāyan)	प्रेम + नारायण (Prem + nārāyan)	2 + 4
भारतभुषण(Bhāratbhushan)	भारत+ भुषण (Bhārat + bhushan)	3 + 3
जनार्दनराव(Janārdhanrāo)	जनार्दन + राव (Janārdhan + rāo)	4 + 2
Number of Aksharas =7		
राजगुरुनगर(Rajgurunagar)	राज+गुरु+नगर(Raj+guru+nagar)	2 + 2 + 3
मनमाधवराव(Manmādhavrāo)	मन+माधव+राव(Man+mādhav+rāo)	2 + 3 + 2
पंढरपुरकर(Pandharpurkar)	पंढर + पुर + कर(Pandharpurkar)	3 + 2 + 2
प्रकाशनारायण(Prakāshnārāyan)	प्रकाश+नारायण(Prakāsh + nārāyan)	3 + 4
गिरिराजकिशोर(Girirājkishor)	गिरिराज + किशोर(Girirāj + kishor)	4 + 3
पुरुषोत्तमदास(Purushottamdās)	पुरुषोत्तम+ दास(Purushottam + dās)	5 + 2
Number of Aksharas =8		
विजयराघवगढ़(Vijayrāghavgarh)	विजय+राघव+गढ़ (Vijay+rāghav+garh)	3 +3 +2
नारायणगावकर(Nārāyangāvkar)	नारायण+गाव+कर(Nārāyan +gāv+kar)	4 +2+ 2
पुरुषोत्तमनगर (Purushottamnagar)	पुरुषोत्तम+नगर (Purushottam+nagar)	5 + 3
त्रिभुवननारायण (Tribhuvannārāyan)	त्रिभुवन+ नारायण (Tribhuvan+nārāyan)	4 + 4

TABLE 8 –Segment Length analysis of Multiword Named Entities

Empirical analysis given in Table 8, confirms that there are always minimum two segments in four to eight aksharas NE. These observations are useful to find out the stressed and unstressed syllables in the multi word NEs which is required to find the break points. These break points are referred to as schwa positions, where the occurrence of ‘a’ vowel is not pronounced and hence deleted.

4.6 Statistical Model

Following terminologies are used in the statistical model

Input: NE in source language is denoted by source word (SW)

Output: NE in the target language as output (English) is denoted by target word (TW).

- SW is divided into the phonetic units called Source Transliteration Units (STUs).
- The TTUs is used to denote Target Transliteration Units (TTU). TTU is equivalent to phonetic unit of English after mapping STU.

- The Devanagari name is represented as a collection of Devanagari phonetic units.
- Name in Devanagari = STU_1, STU_2, ... STU_n }
- The English name is represented as a collection of English phonetic units.
- Name in English = { TTU_1, TTU_2, ... TTU_m }
- WSTU is the weight assigned to a phonetic unit (STU) of the source language.
- WTTU is the weight assigned to a phonetic unit (TTU) of the target language.

If the STU contains any of the vowel matra from [ा, ि ,ी, ु ,ू ,े ,ै,ो,ौ, ं ः] or complete vowel [अ, आ, इ,ई, उ, ऊ, ए,ऐ,ओ,औ] , weight 2 is assigned to it, otherwise weight 1 is assigned. The same weights are mapped to the corresponding TTUs. Weight assignment is represented using mathematical equations (1) and (2).

$$WSTU_i = \begin{cases} 2 \text{ } if\ \exists STU_i \text{ } with\ vowel\ matra\ or\ complete\ vowel \\ 1 \text{ } if\ \exists STU_i \text{ } without\ vowel\ matra \end{cases} \quad (1)$$

$$WTTU_i = \begin{cases} 2 \text{ } if\ \exists TTU_i \text{ } with \text{ [A, e, i, I, o, u, U, ai, au] or preceded by consonant} \\ 1 \text{ } if\ \exists TTU_i \text{ } with \text{ consonant followed by short vowel [a]} \end{cases} \quad (2)$$

where i = 1..n

The probability is calculated for individual phonetic units. As the basis of the method is phonetic model, the probability of mapping STU to TTU is always 1 for the diacritic marks [ा, ि ,ी, ु ,ू ,े ,ै,ो,ौ, ं ः] and complete vowels [अ, आ, इ,ई, उ, ऊ, ए,ऐ,ओ,औ] . When a NE written in Devanagari script is transliterated using English script, the implicit अ attached to the single consonant either gets mapped to 'a' or null depending on the patterns of stress and intonation in a language. The initial probability for all inherent short vowel /a/ is taken as 0.

$$P(STU_i|TTU_i) = \begin{cases} 1 \text{ } if\ \exists TTU_i : TTU_i = WTTU_i = 2 \\ 0 \text{ } if\ \exists TTU_i : TTU_i = WTTU_i = 1 \end{cases} \quad \text{where i = 1..n} \quad (3)$$

If the result of equation (3) is zero for any TTU, then segments are formed (for the NE having aksharas more than 3) if any, and the probability is recalculated for each segment using the TTU position in the word.

$$P(STU_i|TTU_i|WORD\_INITIAL_i) = \begin{cases} 1 \text{ } if\ \exists TTU_i : TTU_i \ \exists 'a' \\ 0 \text{ } if\ \exists TTU_i : TTU_i \ \nexists 'a' \end{cases} \quad \text{where i=1} \quad (4)$$

Ex-Or

$$P(STU_i|TTU_i|WORD\_MEDIAL_i) = \begin{cases} 1 \text{ } if\ \exists TTU_i : TTU_i \ \exists 'a' \\ 0 \text{ } if\ \exists TTU_i : TTU_i \ \nexists 'a' \end{cases} \quad \text{where i=2 to n-1} \quad (5)$$

Ex- Or

$$P(STU_i|TTU_i|WORD\_FINAL_i) = \begin{cases} 1 \text{ } if\ \exists TTU_i : TTU_i \ \nexists 'a' \\ 0 \text{ } if\ \exists TTU_i : TTU_i \ \exists 'a' \end{cases} \quad \text{where i= n} \quad (6)$$

4.7 Segmentation and classification

In our approach, classification is obtained by using the supervised learning approach. Following is the analysis of the named entities in Hindi and Marathi to obtain the classification based on the position and weight of the phonetic entity. Most of the four aksharas named entities are formed with the combination of two different words. As the length of the Devanagari word is 4 and different weights are 2, the possible combinations can be sixteen as shown in Table 9.

SN	Weight Pattern	Segmentation	Named Entity	Segments
1	1111	11 + 11 (2 + 2)	दशरथ (Dashrath)	दश + रथ
2	1121	11 + 21 (2 + 2)	सलमान(Salmān)	सल + मान
3	2111	21 + 11 (2 + 2)	गिरधर(Girdhar)	गिर + धर
4	2121	21 + 21 (2 + 2)	शामराव(Shāmrāo)	शाम + राव
5	1112	11 + 12 (2 + 2)	मनकर्णा(Mankarna)	मन + कर्णा
6	2112	21 + 12 (2 + 2)	शिवदत्त(Shivdatta)	शिव + दत्त
7	1122	11 + 22 (2 + 2)	मनवेंद्र(Manvendra)	मन + वेंद्र
8	2122	21 + 22 (2 + 2)	धृतराष्ट्र(Dhrutrāshtra)	धृत + राष्ट्र
9	1211	12 + 11 (2 + 2)	वरेकर(Varekar)	वरे + कर
10	1221	12 + 21 (2 + 2)	फत्तेलाल(Fattelāl)	फत्ते + लाल
11	2211	22 + 11 (2 + 2)	निलोफर (Nilofar)	निलो + फर
12	1222	12 + 22 (2 + 2)	झकारीया(Zakārīyā)	झका + रीया
13	2221	22 + 21 (2 + 2)	फैजाबाद(Faizābād)	फैजा + बाद
14	1212	12 + 12 (2 + 2)	मनोरमा(Manoramā)	मनो + रमा
15	2212	22 + 12 (2 + 2)	विश्वकर्मा (Vishwakarma)	विश्व +कर्मा
16	2222	22 + 22 (2 + 2)	चंद्रमौली (Chandramaulī)	चंद्र + मौली

TABLE 9 - Weight Patterns for NE of length 4

From Table 9 following two observations, two inferences and two classes are obtained.

Observations from named entities 1 to 8 in Table 9 are

- Weight patterns 1 to 8 have weight 1 at second position.
- The second position has low weight hence the right boundary of the first segment.

Observations from named entities 9 to 16 in Table 9 are

- Weight patterns 9 to 16 have weight 2 at the second position.
- The second position has high weight in the basic pattern.

Inference 1: From a transliteration point of view, for the four aksharas NE, if the weight pattern has weight 1 at second position; it indicates that the NE consists of two segments. In this case, the NE can be divided into two segments of 2 and 2 aksharas, respectively and short vowel 'a' of second akshara which is schwa gets removed.

Inference 2: From a transliteration point of view, for the four aksharas NE, if the weight pattern has weight 2 at the second position, then no segmentation is needed due to high weight.

Classification: *Class I*: Named entities having weight 1 at the second position

Class II: Named entities having weight 2 at the second position

One of the inferences for eight aksharas NE having 3 segments like /विजयराघवगढ़/ is

Inference 3: From a transliteration point of view, for the eight aksharas named entity, if the weight pattern has weights 1211 or 1221 from the position third to the sixth, it indicates that the named entity consists of three segments. In this case, the named entity can be divided into three segments of 3, 3 and 2 aksharas respectively.

Similar analysis is performed for NEs where numbers of aksharas were equal to 5,6,7,8. Summary of the analysis is given in Table 10.

Number of Aksharas	Possible combination	Number of patterns observed	Number of Inferences	Number of classes found
4	16	16	2	2
5	32	24	3	3
6	64	39	4	4
7	128	17	7	7
8	256	8	4	4

TABLE 10 -Summary of Classification

4.8 Transliteration Example

From the statistical analysis of 15224 named entities (Main Data Sources: Voters' list of State of Maharashtra and Atlas of India both of which are available in Marathi/Hindi and English), twenty inferences are drawn. With the help of supervised learning, twenty classes are used for segmentation and finding the schwa identification and deletion. The overall implementation is illustrated by taking the NE of eight aksharas.

Input in Devanagari → विजयराघवगढ़
Phonetic Units in Devanagari→ [वि] [ज] [य] [रा] [घ] [व] [ग] [ढ़]
Phonetic Units in English →[vi][ja][ya][rā][gha][va][ga[][rh]
Weight Assignment (Eq 2) → [2][1][1][2][1][1][1][1]
Initial Probabilities (Eq 3)→[1][0][0][1][0][0][0][0]
Segmentation (Inference 3)→[vi][ja][ya], [rā][gha][va] and [ga][rh] Three Segments
Probabilities (Eq 4,5 and 6) →[1][1][0] , [1][1][0] and [1][0]
Schwa Deletion → Segment ending Schwas
Final Probabilities (Eq 6) → [1][1][1][1][1][1][1][1]
Transliteration in English→ vijayrāghavgarh

5. Experimentation and Results

Table 11 shows the results of the 15224 names transliterated by using phonetic model and statistical approach for segmentation and schwa deletion.

Number of Akshras	Number of Names	Number of Correct Transliteration (Top-1)	Number of Incorrect Transliterations
2	1839	1832 (99.619%)	07 (0.381%)
3	6061	6040 (99.635%)	21 (0.365%)
4	4780	4646 (97.196%)	134 (2.804%)
5	1970	1785 (90.609%)	185 (9.391%)
6	497	442 (88.933%)	55 (11.067%)
7	61	57 (93.442%)	4 (6.558%)
8	16	12 (75%)	4 (25%)
	15224	14814 (97.306%)	410 (2.694%)

TABLE 11 - Results of phonetic model using statistical approach

The results of accuracy (Top-1) for phonetic model using statistical approach are depicted in figure 1.

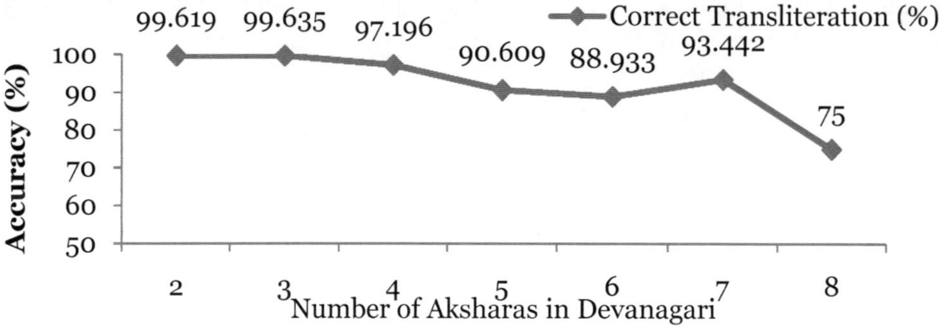

FIGURE 1 - Top-1 Accuracy

Figure 2 depicts the results of Top-1 accuracy, Mean F-Score, Top-2 MRR, Precision and Recall for phonetic model using statistical approach (Li 2009).

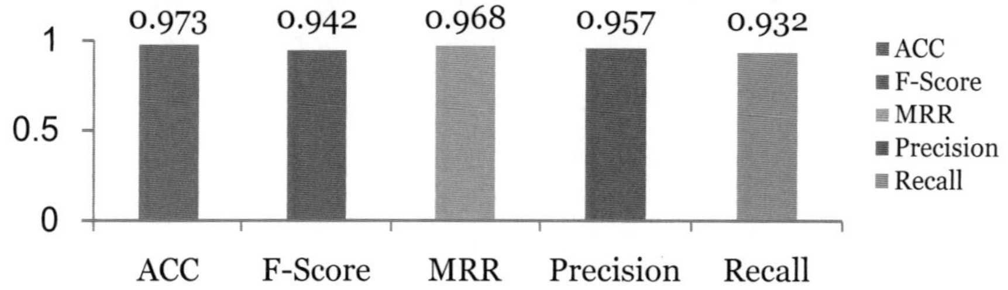

FIGURE 2 - Results Using Performance Metrics

Table 12 is used to generate multiple transliteration candidates (Chinnakotla 2010) .

Hindi	क	ख	ग	ड	व	ई	श	क्ष	औ
English	k,c,q	k,kh	g, gh	d,dh	w,o,b,bh	i,e,ee,ey	sh,s	ksh,x	au,ou

Table 12 : Mapping Table for Multiple Candidates Generation

Conclusion

We presented optimized direct machine transliteration for Hindi to English and Marathi to English language pairs using full consonant approach using only two weights and without corpus. As Hindi and Marathi languages are phonetically rich languages, phonetic based model is used. The accuracy of the transliteration decreases as the length of the Hindi and Marathi named entity increases in terms of number of aksharas. The accuracy of the transliteration decreases if the named entity is made up of multiple smaller length named entities. We showed that, a transliteration system can be built from phonetics, based on local linguistic word formation logic and supervised learning and its accuracy is 97.3%. The phonetic based statistical approach shows the significant improvement in the accuracy for the named entities consisting of four aksharas, five aksharas, six aksharas, seven aksharas and eight aksharas.

References

Al-Onaizan Y, Knight K (2002), Machine translation of names in Arabic text, *Proceedings of the ACL conference workshop on computational approaches to Semitic languages.*

Arbabi M, Fischthal S M, Cheng V C and Bart E (1994), Algorithms for Arabic name transliteration, *IBM Journal of Research and Development*, pp. 183-194.

BIS (1991), Indian standard code for information interchange (ISCII), *Bureau Of Indian Standards*, New Delhi.

Chinnakotla Manoj K., Damani Om P., and Satoskar Avijit (2010), Transliteration for Resource-Scarce Languages, *ACM Trans. Asian Lang. Inform*,Article 14, pp 1-30.

Ekbal A. and Bandyopadhyay S. (2007), A Hidden Markov Model based named entity recognition system: Bengali and Hindi as case studies, *Proceedings of 2nd International conference in Pattern Recognition and Machine Intelligence*, Kolkata, India, pp. 545–552.

Ekbal A. and Bandyopadhyay S. (2008), Bengali named entity recognition using support vector machine, *In Proceedings of the IJCNLP-08 Workshop on NER for South and South East Asian languages*, Hyderabad, India, pp. 51–58.

Ekbal A. and Bandyopadhyay S. (2008), Development of Bengali named entity tagged corpus and its use in NER system, *In Proceedings of the 6th Workshop on Asian Language Resources.*

Ekbal A. and Bandyopadhyay S. (2008), A web-based Bengali news corpus for named entity recognition, *Language Resources & Evaluation*, vol. 42, pp. 173–182.

Ekbal A. and Bandyopadhyay S.(2008), Improving the performance of a NER system by post-processing and voting, *In Proceedings of Joint IAPR International Workshop on Structural Syntactic and Statistical Pattern Recognition*, Orlando, Florida, pp. 831–841.

Ekbal A. and Bandyopadhyay S.(2009), Bengali Named Entity Recognition using Classifier Combination, *In Proceedings of Seventh International Conference on Advances in Pattern Recognition*, pp. 259–262.

Ekbal A. and Bandyopadhyay S. (2009), Voted NER system using appropriate unlabelled data, In *Proceedings of the Named Entities Workshop*, ACL-IJCNLP.

Ekbal A. and Bandyopadhyay S. (2010), Named entity recognition using appropriate unlabeled data, post-processing and voting, *In Informatica*, Volume (34), No. 1, pp. 55-76.

Ganapathiraju M., Balakrishnan M., Balakrishnan N., Reddy R. (2005), .OM: One Tool for Many (Indian) Languages. ICUDL: *International Conference on Universal Digital Library*, Hangzhou.

Ganesh S, Harsha S, Pingali P, and Verma V (2008), Statistical transliteration for cross language information retrieval using HMM alignment and CRF, *In Proceedings of the Workshop on CLIA*, Addressing the Needs of Multilingual Societies.

Jaleel Nasreen Abdul and Larkey Leah S. (2003), Statistical transliteration for English-Arabic cross language information retrieval, *In Proceedings of the 12th international conference on information and knowledge management,* pp: 139 – 146.

Joshi R K, Shroff Keyur and Mudur S P (2003), A Phonemic code based scheme for effective processing of Indian languages, National Centre for Software Technology, Mumbai, *23rd Internationalization and Unicode Conference*, Prague, Czech Republic, pp. 1-17.

Jung S. Y., Hong S., S., Paek E.(2003), English to Korean transliteration model of extended Markov window, *In Proceedings of the 18th Conference on Computational Linguistics*, pp.383–389.

Karimi S, Scholer F, and Turpin(2011), Machine transliteration survey, *ACM Computing Surveys*, Vol. 43, No. 3, Article 17, pp.1-46.

Knight Kevin and Graehl Jonathan (1997), Machine transliteration, *In proceedings of the 35th annual meetings of the Association for Computational Linguistics*, pp. 128-135.

Kopytonenko M. , Lyytinen K. , and Krkkinen T.(2006), Comparison of phonological representations for the grapheme-to-phoneme mapping, In *Constraints* on Spelling Changes: *Fifth International Workshop on Writing Systems*, Nijmegen, The Netherlands.

Koul Omkar N. (2008), Modern Hindi Grammar, Dunwoody Press

Li Haizhou, Kumaran A, Vladimir Pervouchine and Min Zhang (2009), *Report of NEWS 2009 Machine Transliteration Shared Task, ACL-IJCNLP*, pp. 1-19

Malik M.G.A. (2006), Punjabi Machine Transliteration, *Proceedings of the 21st International Conference on Computational Linguistics and the 44th annual meeting of the ACL*, pages 1137–1144.

Martin Jansche and Richard Sproat (2009), Named Entity Transcription with Pair n-Gram Models, *Machine Transliteration Shared Task, ACL-IJCNLP*, pp. 32-35

Mudur S. P., Nayak N., Shanbhag S., and Joshi R. K. (1999), An architecture for the shaping of indic texts, *Computers and Graphics*, vol. 23, pp. 7–24.

Naim R Tyson and Ila Nagar (2009), Prosodic rules for schwa-deletion in Hindi Text-to-Speech synthesis, *International Journal of Speech Technology*, pp. 15–25

Oh Jong-Hoon, Kiyotaka Uchimoto, and Kentaro Torisawa (2009), Machine transliteration using target-language grapheme and phoneme: Multi-engine transliteration approach, Proceedings of the Named Entities Workshop ACL-IJCNLP Suntec, Singapore,AFNLP, pp. 36–39

Padariya Nilesh, Chinnakotla Manoj, Nagesh Ajay, Damani Om P.(2008), Evaluation of Hindi to English, Marathi to English and English to Hindi, *IIT Mumbai CLIR at FIRE.*

Pandey Pramod Kumar (1990), Hindi schwa deletion, Department of Linguistics. South Gujarat University, Surat , lndia, *Lingua* 82, pp. 277-31

Saha Sujan Kumar, Ghosh P. S, Sarkar Sudeshna and Mitra Pabitra (2008), Named entity recognition in Hindi using maximum entropy and transliteration.

Singh Anil Kumar (2006), A computational phonetic model for Indian language scripts, Language Technologies Research Centre International Institute of Information Technology Hyderabad, India.

Sproat R.(2002), Brahmi scripts, In Constraints on Spelling Changes: *Fifth International Workshop on Writing Systems*, Nijmegen, The Netherlands.

Sproat R.(2003), A formal computational analysis of Indic scripts, *In International Symposium on Indic Scripts: Past and Future*, Tokyo.

Sproat R.(2004), A computational theory of writing systems, In Constraints on Spelling Changes: *Fifth International Workshop on Writing Systems*, Nijmegen, The Netherlands.

Stalls Bonnie Glover and Kevin Knight (1998), Translating names and technical terms in Arabic text.

Unicode Standard 5.0 (2007) – Electronic edition, 1991–2007 Unicode, Inc. *Unicode Consortiums*, http://www.unicode.org.

Walambe M. R. (1990), Marathi Shuddalekhan, *Nitin Prakashan*, Pune

Walambe M. R. (1990), Marathi Vyakran, *Nitin Prakashan*, Pune

Selection of Discriminative Features for Translation Texts

Kuo-Ming TANG[1], *Chien-Kang HUANG*[1], *Chia-Ming LEE*[1]
(1) Department of Engineering Science and Ocean Engineering, National Taiwan University, Taipei, Taiwan (R.O.C.)
d965251013@ntu.edu.tw, ckhuang@ntu.edu.tw, trueming@gmail.com

ABSTRACT

Beginning in the first century AD, Buddhist texts underwent a series of translations during a period of nearly 1300 years. The identification of the translator, textual apocrypha, and translation style in Buddhist texts are always important issues. This study proposes an approach to find the most discriminative features that characterize the different Buddhist translation texts or other translation texts. We studied five different kinds of features that can be extracted from translation texts and exploited the F-score and SVM classifier to find the most discriminative features. Not only did we use the translated Buddhist texts, *Kalama Sutta*, for our experiment, but we also chose *The Canterbury Tales* to perform the same experiment and compare the results. According to our experiment results, the newly considered fifth-type features are very effective to identify translators. The selected features will be very useful for further studies of translator characteristics.

KEYWORDS : Feature selection, translator identification, F-score, SVM classifier

Proceedings of the First International Workshop on Optimization Techniques for Human Language Technology, pages 49–64,
COLING 2012, Mumbai, December 2012.

1 Introduction

Translation is an activity to transform linguistic information to another language. Translation as a product that is a written text in a target-language (TL), which represents the result of a translation process, has been described and analysed by a comparison with the respective source-language (SL) text. The relation between the SL text and the TL text had been the object of the numerous and highly abstract models of equivalence (Koller 1978; 21983: 95; Ladmiral 1981: 393). In most cases, these models were prescriptive in nature and of very limited use for the practical translator. Problems in translating are caused at least as much by discrepancies in conceptual and textual grids as by discrepancies in languages.[1] Humankind has been engaged in transforming language for thousands of years, it affects the development of culture and language. "No language can exist unless it is steeped in the context of culture; and no culture can exist which does not have, at its center, the structure of natural language."[2] Translation activities can promote exchanges between different cultures and languages, and it is also very important in the spread and development of religion. For example, efforts to translate The Bible have occurred in Europe and around the world since it was first compiled during the fourth century AD. Translations of The Bible helped many countries to lay the foundation of language. In China, Buddhist texts also experienced a long history of translation during nearly 1300 years from the Eastern Han Dynasty to Song Dynasty (from 25 AD to 1297 AD). Different from the translation of texts from two other major global religions, Christianity and Islam, the translation and interpretation of Buddhist texts has been done with a very open attitude. Therefore, the identification of the translator, textual apocrypha, and translation style in Buddhist texts are particularly important.

This study tries to find the discriminative features in translations of Buddhist texts and other translated texts. Using these features we can set up a training model to identify the translator. Translator identification is a process of examining the characteristics of translation texts to distinguish who is the translator. Similar processes have been used in authorship identification, writing forensics, and similarity detection efforts to statistically analyze literary style. Most of the previous studies addressed the literary-style recognition and authorship analysis problems, which actually initiated this research domain of translation identification. The following sections present related works, the method and procedure, and the experimental evaluation.

2 Related Work

In early studies, researchers analyzed word usage of different authors to identify authors; however, the effectiveness of this approach is limited since word usage is highly dependent on the topic of the article. To achieve generic authorship identification in various applications, it need content free features. In early work, features such as sentence length and vocabulary richness (Yule, 1939 and 1944) were proposed. Later, Burrows (1987) used the high frequency words of occurrence of sets (typically 30 or 50) on *The Federalist Papers*. Holmes (1995) analyzed the use of shorter words. Such word-based and character-based features required intensive efforts in selecting the most appropriate set of words that best distinguished a given set

---

[1] Anton Popovič, 'The Concept of "Shift of Expression" in Translation Analysis' in James Holmes (ed.), *The Nature of Translation* (The Hague and Paris: Mouton, 1970).

[2] Robert Scholes, *Structuralism in Literature* (New Haven: Yale University Press, 1974), p. 10.

of authors (Holmes & Forsyth, 1995), and sometimes those features were not reliable discriminators when applied to a wide range of applications.

Few studies about the translator identification and textual apocrypha can be found in the past. However, there are many important results from the previous studies in authorship identification and literary-style recognition. The most convincing study in the field of authorship identification and literary-style recognition was conducted by Mosteller and Wallace in 1964. They studied the mystery of the authorship of *The Federalist Papers*, and their conclusion was generally accepted by historical scholars and became a milestone in this field.

For many major previous studies in literary-style recognition since the 1960s, lexical and syntactic features were most commonly used as the characteristics of literary-style. The most used approaches were statistical methods and machine-learning techniques. Few researchers have addressed multiple-language issues. These studies are summarized in Table 1.

2.1 Translation Identification

There are no scholarship paper can be found in Translation Identification or Translator Identification. But, the text style detection techniques to identify translator is very similar to Authorship Identification. This study refers to two major techniques for text style detection in Authorship Identification, statistical analysis and machine learning method. In early studies, most analytical tools used in authorship analysis were statistical univariate methods, such as Mosteller and Wallace (1964), Farringdon (1996), and Holmes (1998) . The advent of powerful computers instigated the extensive use of machine learning techniques in authorship analysis, such as Tweedie et al. (1998), Khmelev and Tweedie (2001), De Vel et al. (2001) and Argamon et al. (2003). In general, machine-learning methods achieved higher accuracy than did statistical methods. In Table 1, T1 denotes the use of the technique of statistical analysis and T2 denotes the use of the technique of machine learning.

2.2 Techniques in Identification

Due to the international nature of the Internet, it is important to study authorship identification in a multilingual context, but only Stamatatos et al. (1999 and 2001) conducted authorship identification with multiple languages, analyzing English and Greek newspaper articles. Peng, Schuurmans, Keselj, & Wang (2003) conducted experiments with Greek, English, and Chinese data to examine the performance of authorship attribution across multiple languages. In all three languages, the best accuracy achieved was 90%. However, the performance with Chinese writings was not as good as that with English writings, as shown in Table 1.

Our study is based on those previous studies and uses a machine-learning technique to recognize the translation-style of Buddhist texts. We also propose a framework for translator identification and literary-feature extraction. Machine learning methods have been used to establish an individual translator's translation-style vector-space-based model. According to the identification model, the identity of the translator of Buddhist texts can be clarified in the cases when the identity of the translator has previously been uncertain or unknown.

In order to find the more discriminative text-features, this study adopts an iteration of a feature extraction mechanism. The feature extractor can analyze and extract the text features in texts from the feature vector. After iterating the feature extraction method, the more discriminative text features are found.

Previous studies	Used type of features	Multilanguage	Authors	Training size (# of docs)
(Mosteller & Wallace, 1964)	T1	No	3	85
(Ledger & Merriam, 1994)	T1	No	2	N/A
(Merriam & Matthews, 1994)	T2	No	2	50
(Martindale & McKenzie, 1995)	T1+T2	No	3	85
(Mealand, 1995)	T1	No	1	N/A
(Holmes & Forsyth, 1995)	T1+T2	No	3	85
(Farringdon, 1996)	T1	No	N/A	N/A
(Baayen et al., 1996)	T1	No	2	2
(Tweedie et al., 1996)	T2	No	3	85
(Tweedie & Baayen, 1998)	T1	No	8	16
(Binongo & Smith, 1999)	T1	No	2	5
(Stamatatos et al., 1999)	T1	Yes	10	20
(De Vel et al., 2001)	T2	No	4	1259
(Stamatatos et al., 2001)	T1	Yes	10	300
(Khmelev & Tweedie, 2001)	T2	No	45	380
(Corney et al., 2002)	T2	No	N/A	N/A
(Baayen et al., 2002)	T1	No	8	72
(Peng et al., 2003)	T2	Yes	20	500
(Zheng et al., 2006)	T2	Yes	20	40

TABLE 1 – Previous studies in literary-style recognition and authorship identification. (T1 denotes the technique of statistical analysis and T2 denotes the technique of machine learning)

3 Method

In this study, we reduce the problem of translator identification to a classification problem. A learning classifier is able to learn based on a sample. Statistical methods are used to establish an individual translation-style vector-space-based model, such as Support Vector Machines (SVM), decision trees, etc. However, the focus of this study is not in the classification. The classification model just uses to extract the discriminative text features.

In order to find the more discriminative text features, this study adopts an iterative feature extract method using the F-score measure. The feature extractor can analyze and extract the text features in Buddhist texts, distinguishing them by the classification model. After the iteration of the feature extraction method, the more discriminative text features are found. The procedure for identifying translators by using feature extraction can be divided into three steps, as shown in Figure 1:

Step 1: Corpus Collection

In order to profile the translation styles of each translator and generate a translator identification model, in the first step we need to collect the translated Buddhist texts and a list of potential translators.

Step 2: Feature Extraction

Based on the classification model, the feature extractor analyzes and extracts the features in Buddhist texts. An iteration of feature extraction occurs using the F-score measure to find the more discriminative features. After feature extraction, each unstructured text is represented as a vector of the translation-style features.

Step 3: Model Validation

As done in a typical classifier learning process, the Buddhist text collection is divided into two subsets. One subset, called the training set, is used to train the classification model. The classification techniques applied in this process might lead to models with different predictive powers. The other subset is called the testing set, which is used to cross-validate the prediction power of the translator-identification model generated by the classification model. If the performance of the classifier is verified by the testing set, it can be used to identify the new translations. An iterative training and testing process might be needed to develop a good translator-prediction model.

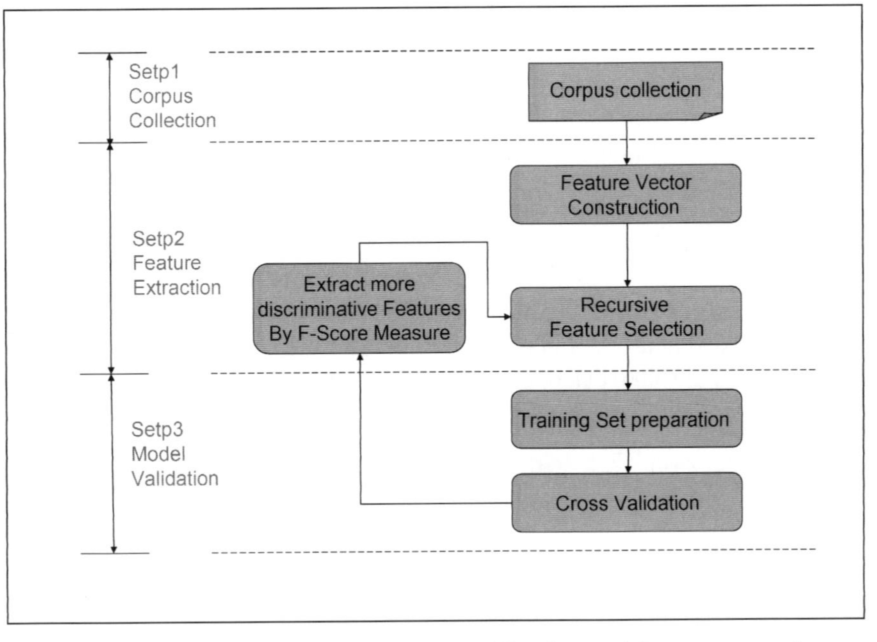

FIGURE 1 – Procedure of translator identification and feature extraction

3.1 Corpus Collection

In "Linguistic Aspects of Translation," Roman Jakobson (1960) distinguishes three types of translation:

1. Intralingual translation or rewording (an interpretation of verbal signs by means of other signs in the same language).
2. Interlingual translation or translation proper (an interpretation of verbal signs by means of some other language).
3. Intersemiotic translation or transmutation (an interpretation of verbal signs by means of signs of nonverbal sign systems).

In the message collection, two important texts must be collected: the original Buddhist texts and the texts of translators.

The main purpose of this study is to identify the translator of Buddhist texts. However, in order to do so, the identification model must be very versatile. Therefore, another literary work—a collection of English tales—was chosen as a testing corpus. For our studies, we used two kinds of translation texts as sample corpora: the *Kalama Sutta* as the Buddhist text and *The Canterbury Tales* as the collection of English tales. Each of these texts are well-known and versions of each have been translated by different translators. There is a difference between these two literary works. The Buddhist text, *Kalama Sutta*, was translated from different languages. However, the English tales, *The Canterbury Tales,* were written in the same language but at different time periods. The background of these two translation texts and their translators is described below.

3.1.1 Buddhist Text

Kalama Sutta is one of training corpora for Buddhist texts in this study. The original sutta is the Pali version, and it was translated into English. The sutta starts off by describing how the Buddha passes through the village of Kesaputta and is greeted by its inhabitants, the Kalamas of the title. They ask for his advice; they say that many wandering holy men and ascetics pass through the village, expounding their teachings and criticizing the teachings of others. So whose teachings should they follow? He delivers in response a sermon that serves as an entry point to the Buddhadhamma for those unconvinced by mere spectacular revelation.

Buddha proceeds to list the criteria by which any sensible person can decide which teachings to accept as true. He tells the Kalamas not to believe religious teachings just because they are claimed to be true or even through the application of various methods or techniques. Direct knowledge grounded in one's own experience can be called upon. He advises that the words of the wise should be heeded and taken into account. Not, in other words, passive acceptance but, rather, constant questioning and personal testing to identify those truths that you are able to demonstrate to yourself actually reduce your own stress or misery.

Two important translators who had translated the Kalama Sutta into English were Thānissaro Bhikkhu (born 1949) and Bodhi Bhikkhu (born 1944). This study used their translations of Buddhist texts to generate a translation-style identification model and find the more discriminative features of their translations.

3.1.2 Canterbury Tales

The Canterbury Tales is a collection of stories written in Middle English by Geoffrey Chaucer at the end of the 14th century. The tales were mostly written in verse, although some are in prose, and they are told as part of a story-telling contest by a group of pilgrims as they travelled together on a journey from Southwark to the shrine of Saint Thomas Becket at the Canterbury Cathedral. The prize for this contest was a free meal at the Tabard Inn at Southwark on their return.

Following a long list of works written earlier in his career, including Troilus and Criseyde, House of Fame, and Parliament of Fowls, the Canterbury Tales was Chaucer's *magnum opus*. He uses the tales and the descriptions of the characters to paint an ironic and critical portrait of contemporary English society and particularly of the Church. Structurally, the collection bears the influence of The Decameron, which Chaucer is said to have come across during his first diplomatic mission to Italy in 1372. However, Chaucer peoples his tales with "sondry folk" rather than Boccaccio's fleeing nobles.

A modernised version or translation was published by A. S. Kline in 2007 that retained Chaucer's rhyme scheme and remained close to the original, but eliminated archaisms that would require explanatory notes. Another version was translated and edited by Gerard NeCastro in 2007. Both of these versions are written in modern English, translated from Middle English.

3.2 Feature Extraction

Most previous studies addressed the authorship identification problem, which actually initiated this research domain. Table 3 summarizes major studies in authorship identification since the 1960s. Lexical and syntactic features were most commonly used. Statistical approaches were extensively used in the past, but more applications of machine learning techniques have been observed recently.

3.2.1 Feature type

Lexical features can be further divided into character-based and word-based features. In our research, we included character-based lexical features used in de Vel (2000), Forsyth and Holmes (1996), and Ledger and Merriam (1994), vocabulary-richness features in Tweedie and Baayen (1998), and word-length-frequency features used in Mendenhall (1887) and de Vel et al. (2000).

Syntactic features, including function words, punctuation, and parts of speech, can capture an author's writing style at the sentence level. The discriminating power of syntactic features is derived from people's different habits of organizing sentences.

Structural features represent the way an author organizes the layout of a piece of writing. De Vel (2000) introduced several structural features specifically for e-mail. Because e-mail contains many general structural features, we adopted those features applicable for online texts. In addition, we added features, such as paragraph indentation and signature-related features. In total, we adopted 14 structured features, including 10 features from de Vel (2000) and four newly proposed features.

Content-specific features are important discriminating features. The selection of such features is dependent on specific application domains.

Translation features include the simplification feature and explicit features, as shown in Table 2.

Features	Label	Content
Lexical features	F1	Average word/sentence length, Vocabulary richness
Syntactic Features	F2	Frequency of function words, Use of punctuation
Structural Features	F3	Paragraph length, Indentation
Content-specific Features	F4	Frequency of keywords
Translation Features	F5	Simplification and explicit features

TABLE 2 – Features of Authorship Identification

3.2.2 Iterative Selection

This paper used the F-score as a feature filter to find the more discriminative features. It is a simple technique that measures the discrimination of two sets of real numbers. Given training vectors x_k, $k = 1,\ldots, m$, if the number of positive and negative instances are n_+ and n_-, respectively, then the F-score of the ith feature is defined as follows (Y.-W. Chen, 2005):

$$F(i) \equiv \frac{(\bar{x}_i^{(+)} - \bar{x}_i)^2 + (\bar{x}_i^{(-)} - \bar{x}_i)^2}{\frac{1}{n_+ - 1}\sum_{k=1}^{n_+}(x_{k,i}^{(+)} - \bar{x}_i^{(+)})^2 + \frac{1}{n_- - 1}\sum_{k=1}^{n_-}(x_{k,i}^{(-)} - \bar{x}_i^{(-)})^2}$$

- $\bar{x}_i$, $\bar{x}_i^{(+)}$, and $\bar{x}_i^{(-)}$ are the average of the *i*th feature of the whole, positive, and negative data sets, respectively.
- $x_{k,i}^{(+)}$ is the *i*th feature of the *k*th positive instance
- $x_{k,i}^{(-)}$ is the *i*th feature of the *k*th negative instance

The numerator indicates the discrimination between the positive and negative sets, and the denominator indicates the one within each of the two sets. The larger the F-score is, the more likely this feature is more discriminative.

There are five steps in this F-score measure:
1. Calculate the F-score of every feature.
2. Pick some possible thresholds to remove low and high F-scores.
3. For each threshold, do the following: Drop features with an F-score below this threshold. Randomly split the training data into Xtrain and Xvalid. Let Xtrain be the new training data. Use the SVM procedure to obtain a predictor; use the predictor to predict Xvalid. Repeat the steps above five times, and then calculate the average validation error.
4. Choose the threshold with the lowest average validation error.
5. Eliminate features with an F-score below the selected threshold.

After the execution of above steps, apply the SVM procedure again.

3.3 Classification Model

This study used a support vector machine (SVM) method as a classification technology. SVM is a set of related supervised learning methods that analyze data and recognize patterns, which can be used for classification and regression analysis. As in a typical classifier learning process, the translation of texts is divided into two subsets. One subset, called the training set, is used to train the classification model. The classification techniques applied in this process might lead to models with different predictive powers. The other subset is called the testing set, which is used to validate the prediction power of the translator-identification model generated by the classification model. If the performance of the classifier is verified by the testing set, it can even be used to identify a new translator. An iterative training and testing process might be needed to develop a good translator-prediction model. This paper uses LIBSVM as an SVM tool. LIBSVM is a set of an integrated software. Components of LIBSVM have different functions: C-SVC and nu-SVC are used for support vector classification, epsilon-SVR and nu-SVR are used for regression, and one-class SVM is used for distribution estimation. It supports multi-class classification.

3.4 Training Set

A classification task usually involves separating data into training and testing sets. Each instance in the training set contains one target value (i.e. the class labels) and several attributes (i.e. the features or observed variables). The goal of SVM is to produce a model (based on the training data) that predicts the target values of the test data given only the test data attributes.

3.5 Cross Validation.

This study uses LIBSVM to find two parameters for an RBF kernel: C and γ automatically. It is not known beforehand which C and γ are best for a given problem; consequently some kind of model selection (parameter search) must be done. The goal is to identify a good set of parameters (C; γ) so that the classifier can accurately predict unknown data (i.e. testing data). It is important to note that it might not be useful to achieve high levels of training accuracy (i.e. a classifier that accurately predicts training data whose class labels are indeed known). A common strategy is to separate the dataset into two parts, of which one is considered unknown. An improved version of this procedure is known as cross-validation. In v-fold cross-validation, we divide the training set into v subsets of equal size. Sequentially one subset is tested using the classifier trained on the remaining v-1 subsets. Thus, each instance of the whole training set is predicted once so the cross-validation accuracy is the percentage of data that are correctly classified.

4 Experiments

4.1 Experimental Design

To examine different features and techniques, we designed several translation identification tasks. First, four feature sets were created. In this case, we use F1, F2, F3, and F4 to denote lexical, syntactic, structural, and content-specific features, respectively. The first feature set contained lexical features (F1) only. Syntactic features were added to F1 to form the second feature set (F1+F2). Structural features were added to form the third feature set (F1+F2+F3). The fourth and fifth feature sets contained four types (F1+F2+F3+F4) and five types (F1+F2+F3+F4+F5) of features, respectively. We chose this incremental method in this order because it represents the evolutionary sequence of style features, and we intended to examine the effect of adding relatively new features to existing ones. Second, we adopted SVM classifiers as the classifiers. A 5-fold cross-validation was used to estimate the accuracy of the classification model.

For this study, we used the Buddhist text corpus, Kalama Sutta, and the English tales corpus, The Canterbury Tales. The basic information about these two corpora is shown in Table 3.

4.2 Experimental Results

Using the SVM classifier, we found that the maximum validation accuracy of Lexical Features (F1) was 68.42% and 100% in the *Kalama Sutta* and *The Canterbury Tales* texts, respectively. The maximum validation accuracy of Syntactic Features (F2) was 86.84% and 100%, respectively. The maximum validation accuracy of Structural Features (F3) was 68.42% and 55.26%, respectively. The maximum validation accuracy of Content-specific Features (F4) was 92.01% and 78.94%, respectively. The maximum validation accuracy of Translation Features (F5) was 89.47% and 100%, respectively. Details are shown in Tables 4 and 5 and in Figure 2.

Item	Kalama Sutta	The Canterbury Tales
Corpus size	38 samples	38 samples
File size	0.6M	1.4M
Number of Samples	38 paragraphs	38 paragraphs
Number of Words	37772	3201248
Size of Vocabulary	798	22875
Average bytes per sample	1069.9	906012.1
Average characters per sample	534.9	45306.1
Training/Testing	5-fold cross validation	5-fold cross validation
Dimensions of feature vector	69	69
Type of classifiers	SVM	SVM

TABLE 3 – Basic information of the translation corpora

Feature sets	Feature sizes	Extracted features sizes	Maximum validation accuracy
F1	14	2	68.42%
F2	81	80	86.84%
F3	6	2	68.42%
F4	231	231	92.10%
F5	28	13	89.47%
F1+F2	95	45	86.84%
F1+F2+F3	101	23	92.10%
F1+F2+F3+F4	332	81	97.36%
F1+F2+F3+F4+F5	360	81	97.36%

TABLE 4 – Maximum validation accuracy for different features of *Kalama Sutta*

Feature sets	Feature sizes	Extracted features sizes	Maximum validation accuracy
F1	14	2	100%
F2	81	80	100%
F3	6	2	55.26%
F4	231	231	78.94%
F5	28	13	100%
F1+F2	95	45	100%
F1+F2+F3	101	23	100%
F1+F2+F3+F4	332	64	100%
F1+F2+F3+F4+F5	360	71	100%

TABLE 5 – Maximum validation accuracy for different features of *The Canterbury Tales*

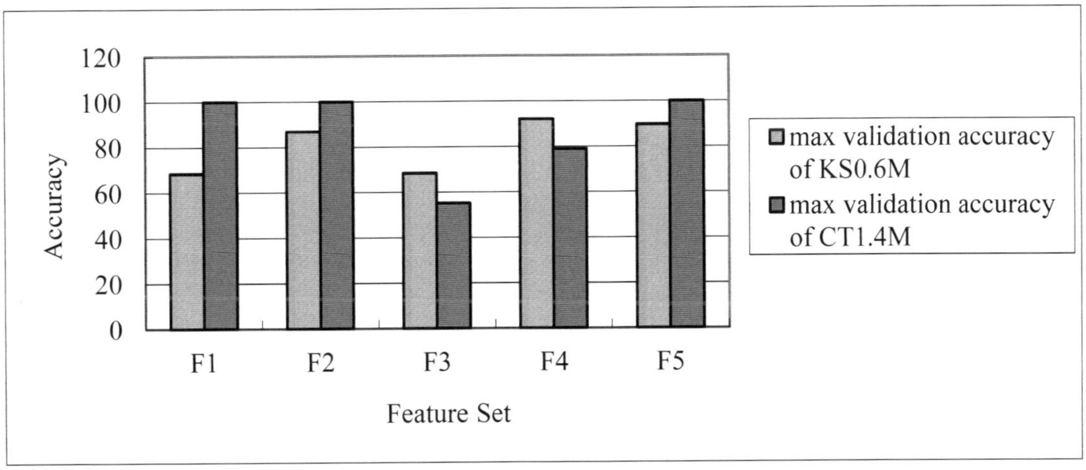

FIGURE 2 – Line chart of the maximum validation accuracy for different features in SVM

As seen in Tables 5 and 6, the best maximum validation accuracy for *Kalama Sutta* is 92.10% in Content-specific Features (F4). However, the maximum validation accuracy for *The Canterbury Tales* is 100% in Lexical Features (F1), Syntactic Features (F2) and Translation Features (F5). For *Kalama Sutta*, although the features F4 performance is relatively good, features F2 and F5 continue to be essential features. For *The Canterbury Tales*, features F4 and F3 are not good, relatively.

There are five combinations of feature sets: F1 (Lexical Features), F1+F2 (Lexical and Syntactic Features), F1+F2+F3 (Lexical, Syntactic, and Structural Features), F1+F2+F3+F4 (Lexical, Syntactic, Structural, and Content-specific Features), and all five features, F1+F2+F3+F4+F5 (Lexical, Syntactic, Structural, Content-specific, and Translation Features). The size of F1 is 14, maximum validation accuracy is 68.42% for *Kalama Sutta*; F1+F2 is 86.84%; and F1+F2+F3 is 92.10%. Both of the maximum validation accuracy values of Features F1+F2+F3+F4 and F1+F2+F3+F4+F5 are 97.36% for *Kalama Sutta*. However, the maximum validation accuracy of all feature combinations is 100% in CT1.4M.

For *Kalama Sutta*, the best maximum validation accuracy from Table 5 is 92.10% in Content-specific Features (F4). Also from Table 5, both of the maximum validation accuracy values of Features F1+F2+F3+F4 and F1+F2+F3+F4+F5 are 97.36%. It can be seen that the Content-specific Features (F4) dominate the results of maximum validation accuracy among all features of the *Kalama Sutta*. However, in *The Canterbury Tales*, the dominant features are Lexical Features (F1), Syntactic Features (F2), and Translation Features (F5), as shown in Table 6. The comparison of maximum validation accuracy values between *Kalama Sutta* and *The Canterbury Tales* is shown in Figure3.

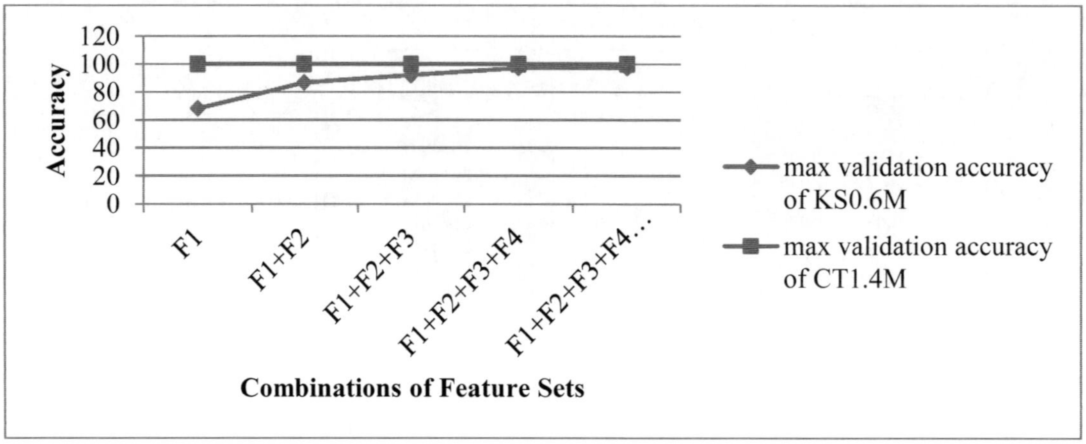

FIGURE 3 – Comparison of maximum validation accuracy values for different feature sets

This study used the F-score measure as a feature filter to find the more discriminative features in different combinations of feature sets. Details are shown in Figure 4.

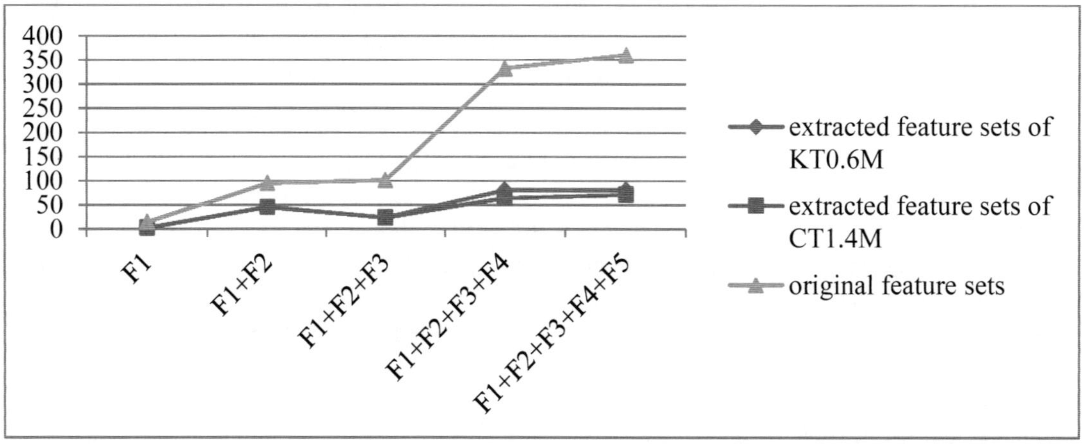

FIGURE 4 – Comparison of the number of extracted features for different feature sets

As shown in Tables 4 and 5 and in Figure 4, the number of F1 features is 14, the number of discriminative features is 2 extracted by the iteration filter in both *Kalama Sutta* and *The Canterbury Tales*. The number of F1+F2 features is 95, and the number of discriminative features extracted by the iteration filter in both corpora is 45. The number of F1+F2+F3 feature is 101, and the number of discriminative features extracted by the iteration filter in both corpora is only 23. The number of F1+F2+F3+F4 feature is 332, and the number of discriminative features extracted by the iteration filter in *Kalama Sutta* is 81. However, the number of discriminative features extracted by the iteration filter in *The Canterbury Tales* is only 64. The number of F1+F2+F3+F4+F5 feature is 360, and the number of discriminative features extracted by the iteration filter in *Kalama Sutta* is also 81 (the same as Feature F1+F2+F3+F4). And, the number of discriminative features extracted by the iteration filter in *The Canterbury Tales* is 71.

5 Conclusion

From the results of our experiment, the Content-specific Features (F4) dominate the results of maximum validation accuracy among all features in *Kalama Sutta*. However, in *The Canterbury Tales*, the dominant features are Lexical Features (F1), Syntactic Features (F2) and Translation Features (F5), as shown in Tables 5 and 6.

Additionally, as seen in Tables 5 and 6 and in Figure 4, the number of discriminative features extracted by the iteration filter in *Kalama Sutta* is 81. Also, the number of discriminative features extracted by the iteration filter in *The Canterbury Tales* is 71. It means that fewer features can effectively discriminate the features in translation texts. The number of discriminative features for *Kalama Sutta* and *The Canterbury Tales* are compared for each feature set in Table 6.

Corpus	Features sizes	F1	F2	F3	F4	F5
Kalama Sutta	81/360	0/14	12/80 (14.8%)	0/6	69/230 (85.2%)	0/28
The Canterbury Tales	71/360	2/14 (2.8%)	25/80 (35.2%)	0/6	41/230 (57.7%)	3/28 (4.3%)

TABLE 6 – Comparison of discriminative features.

The F4 feature set (Content-specific Features) has a great impact in Kalama Sutta. There are 69 discriminative features selected from all 230 F4 features (about 85.2%). However, it has less impact in *The Canterbury Tales*; only 41 discriminative features were selected from all 230 F4 features (which still accounts for 57.7%).

There are 81 more discriminative features extracted from feature sets F2 and F4. We can identify these features in *Kalama Sutta*. The content of the F4 feature set (Content-specific Features) in *Kalama Sutta* can be divided into Proper Noun and Adjective, and further analyzed. In the same way, we can also use 71 more discriminative features extracted from F1, F2, F4, and F5 to identify the translation text of The Canterbury Tales.

In future, using the discriminative features, we can develop an authorship-identification model to be used in the prediction of the authorship of unknown translation texts. The result of authorship identification will help the investigator focus his or her efforts on a small set of texts and authors. More formally, a support vector machine constructs a hyper-plane or set of hyper-planes in a high or infinite dimensional space, which can be used for classification, regression, or other tasks. Intuitively, a good separation is achieved by the hyper-plane that has the largest distance to the nearest training data points of any class (so-called functional margin), because in general the larger the margin, the lower the generalization error of the classifier.

Acknowledgments

The authors would like to thank the National Science Council of the Republic of China, Taiwan, for financially supporting this research under Contract No. NSC 99-2410-H-002-203-MY2.

Reference

Anton Popovič. 1970. "The Concept of "Shift of Expression" in Translation Analysis'". *Shift of Expression-in Translation Analysis", James S. Holmes et al*: 78–87.
Argamon, S., M. Koppel, J. Fine & A. R Shimoni. 2003. "Gender, genre, and writing style in formal written texts". *TEXT-THE HAGUE THEN AMSTERDAM THEN BERLIN-* 23 (3): 321–346.
Argamon, S., M. Šarić 及 S. S Stein. 2003. "Style mining of electronic messages for multiple authorship discrimination: first results". in *Proceedings of the ninth ACM SIGKDD international conference on Knowledge discovery and data mining*, 475–480.
Baayen, H., H. van Halteren, A. Neijt & F. Tweedie. 2002. "An experiment in authorship attribution". in *6th JADT.*
Binongo, J. N.G, & M. W. A. Smith. 1999. "The application of principal component analysis to stylometry". *Literary and Linguistic Computing* 14 (4): 445.
Burrows, J. F., & J. F. Burrows. 1987. *Computation into criticism: A study of Jane Austen's novels and an experiment in method.* Clarendon Press Oxford. http://www.getcited.org/pub/102535837.
Carney, D. M, & R. H Nguyen. 2002. *Method and apparatus for adjusting an interval of polling a network printer based on changes in working status of the network printer*. Google Patents.
Chen, Y. W, & C. J Lin. 2006. "Combining SVMs with various feature selection strategies". *Feature Extraction*: 315–324.
Farringdon, J. M, A. Q. Morton, M. G Farringdon & M. D. Baker. 1996. *Analysing for Authorship: A Guide to the Cusum Technique*. University of Wales Press, Cardiff.
Grzybek, P. 2006. "History and methodology of word length studies". *Contributions to the Science of Text and Language*: 15–90.
Holmes, D. I, & R. S Forsyth. 1995. "The Federalist revisited: New directions in authorship attribution". *Literary and Linguistic Computing* 10 (2): 111.
Holmes, D. I. 1998. "The evolution of stylometry in humanities scholarship". *Literary and linguistic computing* 13 (3): 111–117.
Jakobson, R. 1960. "Closing statement: Linguistics and poetics". *Style in language* 350: 377.
Khmelev, D. V, & F. J Tweedie. 2001. "Using Markov Chains for Identification of Writer". *Literary and linguistic computing* 16 (3): 299.
Koppel, M., & J. Schler. 2003. "Exploiting stylistic idiosyncrasies for authorship attribution". in *Proceedings of IJCAI*, 3:69–72.
Koppel, M., J. Schler, S. Argamon & E. Messeri. 2006. "Authorship attribution with thousands of candidate authors". in *Proceedings of the 29th annual international ACM SIGIR conference on Research and development in information retrieval*, 659–660.
Ledger, G., & T. Merriam. 1994. "Shakespeare, Fletcher, and the two noble kinsmen". *Literary and Linguistic Computing* 9 (3): 235.
Martindale, C., & D. McKenzie. 1995. "On the utility of content analysis in author attribution: The Federalist". *Computers and the Humanities* 29 (4): 259–270.
McCarthy, P. M, G. A Lewis, D. F Dufty & D. S McNamara. 2006. "Analyzing writing styles with Coh-Metrix". in *Proceedings of the Florida Artificial Intelligence Research Society International Conference (FLAIRS)*, 764–769.
Mealand, D. L. 1995. "Correspondence analysis of Luke". *Literary and linguistic computing* 10 (3): 171.

Merriam, T. V.N, & R. A.J Matthews. 1994. "Neural computation in stylometry II: An application to the works of Shakespeare and Marlowe". *Literary and Linguistic Computing* 9 (1): 1.
Mosteller, F., & D. Wallace. 1964. "Inference and disputed authorship: The Federalist」.
Oberlander, J., & S. Nowson. 2006. "Whose thumb is it anyway?: classifying author personality from weblog text". in *Proceedings of the COLING/ACL on Main conference poster sessions*, 627–634.
Peng, F., D. Schuurmans, S. Wang & V. Keselj. 2003. "Language independent authorship attribution using character level language models". in *Proceedings of the tenth conference on European chapter of the Association for Computational Linguistics-Volume 1*, 267–274.
Pruscha, H. 1998. "Statistical models for vocabulary and text length with an application to the NT corpus". *Literary and linguistic computing* 13 (4): 195.
Stamatatos, E., N. Fakotakis & G. Kokkinakis. 1999. "Automatic authorship attribution". in *Proceedings of the ninth conference on European chapter of the Association for Computational Linguistics*, 158–164.
Stamatatos, E. 2000. "Text genre detection using common word frequencies". in *Proceedings of the 18th conference on Computational linguistics-Volume 2*, 808–814.
Stamatatos, E. 2001. "Computer-based authorship attribution without lexical measures". *Computers and the Humanities* 35 (2): 193–214.
Tweedie, F. J, & R. H Baayen. 1998. "How variable may a constant be? Measures of lexical richness in perspective". *Computers and the Humanities* 32 (5): 323–352.
De Vel, O., A. Anderson, M. Corney & G. Mohay. 2001. "Mining e-mail content for author identification forensics". *ACM Sigmod Record* 30 (4): 55–64.
Yule, G. U. 1939. "On sentence-length as a statistical characteristic of style in prose: With application to two cases of disputed authorship". *Biometrika* 30 (3/4): 363–390.
Zheng, R., J. Li, H. Chen & Z. Huang. 2006. "A framework for authorship identification of online messages: Writing-style features and classification techniques". *Journal of the American Society for Information Science and Technology* 57 (3): 378–393.

Semi-supervised Learning of Naive Bayes Classifier with feature constraints

Nagesh Bhattu, D.V.L.N.Somayajulu
Department of Computer Science and Engineering
National Institute of Technology Warangal-506004
INDIA
nageshbhattu@gmail.com, soma@nitw.ac.in

ABSTRACT
Semi-supervised learning methods address the problem of building classifiers when labeled data is scarce. Text classification is often augmented by rich set of labeled features representing a particular class. As tuple level labling is resource consuming, semi-supervised and weakly supervised learning methods are explored recently. Compared to labeling data instances (documents), feature labeling takes much less effort and time. Posterior regularization (PR) is a framework recently proposed for incorporating bias in the form prior knowledge into posterior for the label. Our work focuses on incorporating labeled features into a naive bayes classifier in a semi-supervised setting using PR. Generative learning approaches utilize the unlabeled data more effectively compared to discriminative approaches in a semi-supervised setup. In the current study we formulate a classification method which uses the labeled features as constraints for the posterior in a semi-supervised generative learning setting. Our empirical study shows that performance gains are significant compared to an approach solely based on Generelized Expectation(GE) or limited amount of labeled data alone. We also show an application of our framework in a transfer learning setup for text classification. As we allow labeled data as well as labeled features to be used, our setup allows the presence of limited amount of labeled data on the target side of transfer learning where feature constraints are used for transferring knowledge from source domain to target domain.

KEYWORDS: Classification,Posterior Regularization.

Proceedings of the First International Workshop on Optimization Techniques for Human Language Technology, pages 65–78,
COLING 2012, Mumbai, December 2012.

1 Introduction

Semi-supervised learning methods (O. Chapelle and Zien, 2006) address the difficulties of integration of information contained in labeled data and unlabeled data. Though labeled data is scarce, unlabeled data is abundantly available. The success of Semi-supervised methods is based on the premise of using the hidden structure of unlabeled data and aligning it with the limited amount of labeled data. Apart from unlabeled data, there are auxiliary forms of information in the form of labeled features. For example, sentiment analysis which focuses on sentiment classification is often leveraged with sentiment lexicon, which contains prior sentiment orientation of commonly occurring words. They can be used as prior knowledge in building the classifiers. Such auxiliary information has to be incorporated in the form of bias into the learning algorithm.

Though there have been efforts to build informative priors (Raina et al., 2006) or lexicon based classifiers in (Melville et al., 2009), they have been of limited success and often interact with the model in complex ways. Recently there have been research efforts from multiple perspectives addressing the same issue. Generalized Expectation Criteria (GE) is one such approach for regularizing the model based on rich set of constraints. GE allows us to specify global constraints which are allowed to be arbitrary combinations of features.

(Druck et al., 2008) used GE for building classifier solely based on labeled features. But one of the problems encountered while using GE criteria is, the model parameters and constraint parameters when exist together in a semi-supervised setup, increases the computational complexity of the algorithm. (Bellare et al., 2009) and (Druck and McCallum, 2010) addressed this issue using alternative projections approach, which is an extension of EM to discriminative learning methods. Another approach for parameter estimation which is developed simultaneously is Posterior Regularization framework (Ganchev et al., 2010) which is initially proposed for generative learning methods (Graça et al., 2007). In the initial framework in (Graça et al., 2007), constraints chosen were of limited expressibility (instance based).

1.1 Generative vs Discriminative

Generative approaches solve the inference problem modeling the joint distribution of dependent and independent variables. Discriminative methods directly model the conditional of the objective. Previous research by (Ng and Jordan, 2002) indicated that generative approaches outperform discriminative when limited amount of labeled examples are present and may under perform discriminative approaches given large amount of labeled data. Particularly in a semi-supervised setting as observed by (Nigam, 2001) where the unlabeled data is also taken while learning, generative methods shown promising results as they maximize both conditional as well model marginal together.

They proved this in the context of text classification using Multinomial Naive Bayes (MNB) approach. This view is further strengthened by recent work by (Su et al., 2011). In an another work (Druck and McCallum, 2010) has shown how discriminatively constrained generative models based on HMM, can benefit in a semi-supervised learning setup for sequence labeling task. We use PR framework for building a naive bayes classifier using feature labels as well as labeled tuples.

1.2 Transfer Learning

Transfer Learning approaches also address the issue of learning from unlabeled data using labeled data of a related domain. Such approaches are very effective in the context of widespread use of social networks which require text classification as the basic primitive. (Dai et al., 2007) has shown a method of transferring naive bayes classifier using KL-Divergence of source and target domains. A detailed survey of transfer learning approaches is addressed in (Pan and Yang, 2010). In this work we will go through an approach for transfer learning where transfer happens through feature constraints from labeled source domain to target domain. Our framework allows seamless integration of domain knowledge in the form of feature constraints, labeled data as well other domains which have abundant labeled data. Our contributions include constraining naive bayes with feature expectations and simplifying the transfer learning problem seamlessly in a semi-supervised setup.

2 Related Work

Feature prior induction into the model has been studied by (Druck et al., 2008). Work done by (Liu et al., 2004) is one of the earlier efforts for using labeled features in (classification) sentiment analysis. They use paradigm words for each class and prepare a model document for each class and compare geometric similarity of unlabeled documents with these documents for training an EM algorithm. (Melville et al., 2009) used a similar approach where he made a generative assumption of all class specific features being equally likely to appear in their respective class specific documents and all the other words being equally likely to appear in any document. They call this Lexical Classifier and pool multinomials from both lexical classifier as well as MNB from limited amount of labeled data. The prior they induce is rather less intuitive and user does not have much ease in controlling the prior. In the present method discussed in this paper, the prior can be fine-tuned and gives best results when domain expert gives exact prior knowledge.

Topic models presented by (Blei et al., 2003) using Latent Dirichlet Allocation (LDA) are used for inferring the latent topic structure hidden in the document distribution. It is totally unsupervised approach, hence LDA topic based features can be used as prior knowledge for our algorithm. Recently (Lin and He, 2009) used topic models for sentiment analysis. They further used GE expressions to bias the classifier based on sentiment lexicon. It is very effective in the context of sentiment analysis, as the presence of certain words surely effects the sentiment of entire document in one way or other. But they used GE terms along with Sentiment enhanced LDA model with regularization. In a study by (Druck et al., 2009) they have shown how the optimization problem gets complicated with the presence of GE parameters and model parameters in a semi-supervised setup. They have used Dynamic Programming to compute the covariance among the GE parameters and model parameters from labeled data. (Lin and He, 2009) don't use such approach, it is not well defined way of integrating GE terms with the generative model. In a similar context, (Mann and McCallum, 2010) have shown label regularization can be safely added in a semi-supervised setting. But it's use is limited.

Addressing the difficulties of semi-supervised learning with GE, (Bellare et al., 2009) has introduced the method of alternate projections. They use EM algorithm in a discriminative setup. They take two kinds of projections I-Projection and M-Projection which are computationally intensive. But we prefer a generative approach so as to take the benefit of document-word distribution which are even present in a unlabeled corpus. (Su et al., 2011) points out that the traditional EM formulation as given by (Nigam, 2001) reduces the conditional likelihood of the model learnt from the labeled data. They avoid this problem in a rather efficient way which avoids the iterative procedure of EM and prove their results over large of amount of text-classification datasets. There are other methods (Sindhwani et al., 2008) which make use of graph laplacian successfully in a semi-supervised setup using Co-Clustering. These methods are computationally intensive and our method is simpler as we just use a unified constrained learning. As co-clustering methods model the higher order co-occurrences well they show performance gains at the cost of more computation. As in the current work our emphasis is on modeling a unified framework for learning from features and labels, we don't consider laplacian regularization anymore. As Naive Bayes method is generative, (Druck et al., 2007) has first described the method for building a hybrid classifier based on generative and descriminative pair, to fix the bias of generative learning. (Fujino et al., 2008) has given a method for building a hybrid classifier maximizing the joint likelihood of generative and discriminative classifiers. But the method need not converge to a stationary point as the two objectives are different. In our current work, we rather use expectation constraints over unlabeled data. So it is possible to express the optimization function as a single objective function.

(Pan and Yang, 2010) has given a detailed survey of transfer learning methods. In one of their works (Pan et al., 2010) they show a novel method of constructing a graph of domain-independent and domain-dependent features and show how spectral clustering can be used for effective domain adaptation. As part of our transfer learning application we don't consider building a graph, and hence use simple features based on mutual information. Our results are comparable to that of (Blitzer, 2008) with out spending any extra effort in dimensionality reduction. (Ganchev et al., 2010) have also addressed the problem of transfer learning using multi-view learning using agreement constraints between the views. Our approach is to develop a semi-supervised framework where we have feature transfer from related domain in the form of expectation constraints and some labeled training data. (**?**) have shown a method for transfer learning using hybrid generative/discriminative framework. It again suffers from convergence issues as two different objectives are combined.

3 Preliminaries

MNB method has been used for text classification because of it's simplicity. In a semi-supervised learning setup where learning has to be performed with limited labeled data and abundant unlabeled data Naive Bayes approach found it's application as it accounts for the marginal distribution over unlabeled data into it's objective. (Nigam, 2001) found that expectation maximization (EM) algorithm (Dempster et al., 1977) can be successfully applied in the semi-supervised context, treating missing labels of unlabeled data as latent variables of EM. We will now review the Naive Bayes approach.

3.1 Multinomial Naive Bayes

We assume $\mathscr{D}$ denote the set of documents and $\mathscr{V}$ defines the vocabulary of words. Let $\mathscr{Y}$ be set of labels. In the supervised learning setting, where $|\mathscr{D}|$ documents are given, MNB solves the following inference problem by maximum likelihood.

$$p(y|x) \propto p(x|y)p(y)$$

and $p(x|y)$ factors nicely into

$$p(x|y) = \prod_{w_i \in x} p(w_i|y)$$

The parameters of the model are computed as

$$p(w_i|y) = \frac{N_{yi} + \delta}{\sum_i N_{yi} + |\mathcal{V}|\delta}$$

where δ is used for avoiding zero probabilities (known as Lidstone smothing). If we disregard the smoothing, the above probability is simply the empirical ratio of a particular word's frequency compared to sum of all words frequencies appearing over the set of documents of the class.

$$p(w_i|y) = \frac{N_{yi}}{\sum_j N_{yj}}$$

$$N_{yi} = \sum_{t=1}^{|D|} f_{yi}^{t}$$

3.2 Semi-supervised learnig

Classification accuracy depends on the amount of training data available while building the classifier. In a semi-supervised learning setting we assume that in addition to the labeled training data $\mathcal{D}_{\mathcal{L}}$ we also have large amount of unlabeled data $\mathcal{D}_{\mathcal{U}}$ ($|\mathcal{D}_{\mathcal{L}}| << |\mathcal{D}_{\mathcal{U}}|$). As the joint likelihood of the labeled and unlabeled data is not in closed form, EM (Dempster et al., 1977) can be applied which results in the following iterative procedure. The algorithm starts by inferring model parameters from limited amount of labeled data and uses these parameters for inferring probabilistic labels for each of the unlabeled documents in E-step. M-step consists of inferring the parameters using these probabilistic labels for unlabeled document and labels for labeled documents.

$$Initial : \theta_L^0 = \arg\max_{\theta} \sum_{x \in \mathcal{D}_{\mathcal{L}}} log p_{\theta}(x.y)$$

$$EStep : \forall_{x \in \mathcal{D}_{\mathcal{L}} \cup \mathcal{D}_{\mathcal{U}}} compute p_{\theta_t}(y|x)$$

$$MStep : \theta_{t+1} = \arg\max_{\theta} \sum_{x \in \mathcal{D}_{\mathcal{L}} U \mathcal{D}_{\mathcal{U}}} log P_{\theta_t}(x, y).$$

$$N_{yi} = \sum_{x \in \mathcal{D}_{\mathcal{U}}} f_i^x P_{\theta_t}(y|x)$$

The Expectation and Maximization steps are repeated till convergence. N_{yi} is denominator in deciding the probability of feature(word) f_i being in class y (For simplicity we have omitted the terms from labeled data $\mathscr{D}_{\mathscr{L}}$). f_i^x gives the count of feature in document x. (Su et al., 2011) showed how conditional estimates of $P(y|x)$ from labeled data improves both accuracy and performance of naive bayes approach. θ_t gives the current estimates of the parameters for the model. The modified approach of (Su et al., 2011) computes N_{yi} is computed as follows

$$N_{yi} = P_{\theta_t^l}(y|x) \sum_{x \in \mathscr{D}_{\mathscr{U}} \cup \mathscr{D}_{\mathscr{L}}} f_i^x$$

Here θ_t^l are the parameters learnt from $\mathscr{D}_{\mathscr{L}}$.

3.3 Learning From Labeled Features

As suggested by (Druck et al., 2008), it is far easier to label features than labelling documents. They have suggested a method for learning from features using Kullback Liebler (KL) constraints (GE) on feature expectations. Their approach is based on discriminative log-linear models. The objective is given as below.

$$G(f_k) = KL(\hat{f}_k, E_U(E_{p_\theta(y/x)} f_k))$$

$$\mathcal{O} = -\sum_k G(f_k) - \sum_i \frac{\theta_i^2}{2\sigma^2}$$

Here G is GE objective function which evaluates the expectation of conditional given a document has the constraint feature. But discriminative methods can not leverage the marginal word distributions over documents, as they directly maximize the likelihood of $p(y|x)$. In one of their later studies, (Druck and McCallum, 2010) have used both discriminative and generative approaches to get the advantages of both.

4 Expectation Maximization and Posterior Constraints

In this section we review an alternate view of expectation maximization as given in (Neal and Hinton, 1993). We are given a problem of modeling a distribution of x,z where x is observed data and z is unobserved or latent(here we use z instead of y for explicitly distinguishing observed and unobserved and also to be in sync with notation widely used in literature). In the document classification task, unobserved are missing labels for unlabeled documents. Given a sample S = $x_1, ..., x_n$ observed instances of data. EM maximizes the likelihood of $p_\theta(x)$ using two block ascent steps.

$$E : q^{t+1}(z|x) = \arg\min_{q(z|x)} KL(q(z|x) || p_{\theta^t}(z|x)) = p_{\theta^t}(z|x) \quad (1)$$

$$M : \theta^{t+1} = \arg\min_{\theta} E_S \left[\sum_z q^{t+1}(z|x) log p_\theta(x,z) \right]. \quad (2)$$

As suggested by (Ganchev et al., 2010) this view of EM allows us to add constraints over the posterior. Instead of directly using $p_{\theta^t}(z|x)$ we can constrain the posterior to some set $\mathcal{Q}$ (set of constrained posteriors). Their work addressed the induction of instance based constraints for word alignment. The constrained E step looks as follows.

$$E : q^{t+1}(z|x) = \underset{q(z|x)\in\mathcal{Q}}{\arg\min} KL(q(z|x)||p_{\theta^t}(z|x)) \tag{3}$$

The affine constraints used by them are of the form $E_q[f(x,z)] \leq b$. Multiple such constraints are stacked into a vector $\mathbf{E_q}[\mathbf{f}(\mathbf{x},\mathbf{z})] \leq \mathbf{b}$ and it now looks like

$$E : q^{t+1}(z|x) = \underset{q}{\arg\min} KL(q(z|x)||p_{\theta^t}(z|x)) s.t \mathbf{E_q}[\mathbf{f}(\mathbf{x},\mathbf{z})] \leq \mathbf{b}. \tag{4}$$

It is proved in (Graça et al., 2007) that local maximum of this constrained EM is indeed local maximum of regularized likelihood. Instead of these constraints we can use any convex constraints which has the effect of changing the regularization term. If we use $L2$ constraints then it is equivalent to solving the same optimization problem with L2 regularization.

4.1 Feature Expectation Constraints

(Druck et al., 2008) has first shown the utility of feature constrained learning. The constraints specify our prior belief about the presence of certain words strongly biasing the class of the document. For example the presence of word 'puck' strongly indicative of document being about hockey. If we know that 90% of documents which contain 'puck' are of class 'hockey', then we can express our constraint as 0.90N documents should have class 'hockey' (where N is the number of all the documents which contain 'puck'). We can specify the same using the following L2 based constraint.

$$\frac{1}{2\beta}\left\|\hat{f}_y - \sum_j [f(w_j, y)]\right\|_2^2 \tag{5}$$

Here $\hat{f}_y$ is feature expectation of a feature f and summation on the right runs over all the documents counting the number of documents containing feature f. It's conjugate is $-\mu'\hat{f}_y + \frac{\beta}{2}\left\|\mu\right\|_2^2$. The conjugates of various convex functions and fenchel's duality are well treated in (Dudík, 2007).

4.2 Modified EM approach

In our problem we have k L2 constraints of the above type and we use these constraints for learning from unlabeled data. The set $\mathcal{Q}$ represents the distributions constrained by these k constraints. So we have to find the auxiliary distribution $q(z|x)$ which has minimum KL divergence with $p_{\theta^t}(z|x)$ subjected to q restricted to $\mathcal{Q}$. This is similar to Maximum Entropy principle of discriminative approaches. This is called I-Projection and it is used in (Graça et al., 2007), (Druck and McCallum, 2010), (Bellare et al., 2009) in a similar setting. The dual form of complete objective is

$$\mu^{(t+1)} = \underset{\mu}{\arg\max}\, \mu'\hat{f} - \sum_z p_{\theta^t}(z|x) exp(\mu' f(z,x)) - \frac{\beta}{2}\left\|\mu\right\|_2^2 \tag{6}$$

Here β is a regularization constant. μ is a vector of parameters for the constraints. $\hat{f}$ is a vector of feature expectations. Here at $\mu*$ of the above objective function, the distribution $q_{\mu*}$ where $q_\mu(z|x) \propto p_{\theta^t}(z|x)exp(\mu' f(z,x))$ gives the optimal constrained distribution we are looking for. The gradient of this objective is $\hat{f} - E_{q_\mu}[f(x,z)] - \beta\mu$. We solve this using L-BFGS which is a general purpose unconstrained optimization procedure. The complexity of each step of the EM algorithm is the cost of normal E step using MNB and the cost of constrained objective over the unlabeled data. If the unlabeled data is more L-BFGS might take longer time to converge to a optimal solution. Stochastic gradient descent method can be used in our objective for faster convergence. The M Step of the algorithm remains simple as we are using MNB. Computing the updated parameters of the M step uses $q^{t+1}(z|x)$ instead of $p(z|x)$.

5 Transfer Learning using Constraints

There are few efforts of transfer learning (Pan et al., 2010) (Dai et al., 2007) (Tan et al., 2009). In this section we will see how our method of constrained naive bayes is useful in building a simple scheme for transfer learning(TL). Finding the domain independent features is the key for the success of transfer learning approach. In a transfer learning setup we have labeled data only on the source side and the objective is to transfer the knowledge of inference from source task to target task(where no labeled data is available). In many TL tasks low dimensional embedding is factored out from the labeled source data and unlabeled target data. Letter this embedding is used along with source-domain classifier to do the target classification. In our framework we can figure out useful features for transfer learning and compute the feature expectations of these features in the source domain. If the features selected are informative for transfer learning, the feature expectations will behave similarly in the target domain. This allows us to transfer knowledge in a semi-supervised setup. So we can use the feature constraints learnt from a related domain to be used in target domain where only limited amount of supervision is available in the form of labeled features or labeled instances.

5.1 Method

Let $\mathscr{D}_{\mathscr{S}}$ and $\mathscr{D}_{\mathscr{T}}$ be source and target domains of our interest. $\mathscr{D}_{\mathscr{S}}$ consists of labeled documents (x,y) where $x \in \mathscr{X}$ document space and $y \in \mathscr{Y}$ label space. The target domain consists of documents (x) where $x \in \mathscr{X}$. Though they come from the same document space (vocabulary). The mutual information(MI) of a feature f_i with respect to the labels $\mathscr{Y}$ is

$$MI(f_i) = \sum_{y \in \mathscr{Y}} p(f_i, y) ln\left(\frac{p(f_i, y)}{(p(f_i) * p(y))}\right) \quad (7)$$

We select features of highest mutual information which occur in both domains. Though there are other methods of selecting informative features, we found this method giving better results.

6 Experiments

We evaluate our algorithm on 5 datasets which are previously used by Gregory Druck at.al (Druck et al., 2008). We further divide the dataset into binary classification problems. For datasets involving more than two classes we use multi-class classification. We use 65/35

[1] http://www.umass.edu/ mccallum/code-data.html

[2] http://www.cs.waikato.ac.nz/ml/weka/

[3] http://cs.cmu.edu/ webkb

Table 1: Datasets Description

NameOfDataset	Description	
20 newsgroups(20NG) [1]	20000 instances	20 classes
Ohscal [2]	111162 instances	10 classes
SRAA	73,218 instances	4 classes
WebKB [3]	4199 instances	4 classes
News3	9,558 instances	44 classes

training/test split through out our experiments. We took 20 news group, sraa and webkb from the same source as that of (Druck et al., 2008). Ohscal and News3 represent classification problems with large number of classes. They are taken from [2] and [3] respectively. We use information gain to simulate a human-expert providing us the labeled features.

6.1 BaseLine Approaches

We use EM-MNB as the base-line approach for semi-supervised learning. We also use GE-FL as the baseline classifier based on Druck's implementation. A semi-supervised learning algorithm leveraging labeled features and labeled data is called EM-FL (EM with Feature Labaling). The labeled features for the classification are learnt using mutual information. 1 to 16 labeled features are used for each class.

6.2 Comparison with Base Line Approaches

Together with the labeled features we also use some labeled examples. We used mallet library for our implementation. It has GE-FL and EM-MNB implemented in it. We vary the number of labeled examples among 1,2,4,8,16 per class. As the number of labeled examples increases, our algorithm's performance asymptotically approaches that of EM-MNB (unless the labeled features contain some information not expressed in the labeled tuples) . But when labeled examples are scarce, our method takes the benefit of labeled features and performs all the time better than EM-MNB by large amount. Each of the experiments are repeated for 10 runs and the average accuracy is reported. On 20 News and WebKB datasets, EM-FL fared significantly better than GE-FL. On sraa and new3 datasets, GE-FL fared better than EM-FL. The reason for this behavior is, GE-FL learns it's model based on limited number of feature constraints. The parameters of the model for features not in the constraint set estimated based on their co-occurrence with the constraint features. In our model, we have to cope with labeled features as well as labeled examples, so when the feature constraints carry more information GE-FL outperforms our approach. The two parameters of EM-FL are weight for unlabeled data and gaussian prior variance. The optimal parameters are found by using a grid search of possible values for these parameters with values between 0.1 to 1.5 with in a span of 0.1 and optimal values are used for each of our experiments. For the ohscal dataset EM algorithm fared well. This is because of the amount of unlabeled data available for learning. But EM-FL is also closer and infact fared better than EM when the number of labeled examples per class is lesser.

[4] http://mallet.cs.umass.edu

Dataset	Algo	Number of Labeled Examples per class				
		1	2	4	8	16
20 News	EM-FL	71.5(1.51)	71.59(1.53)	71.83(1.35)	71.92(1.39)	**72.53(1.53)**
	EM	14.29(5.15)	19.22(3.62)	21.02(4.38)	25.5(7.47)	29.98(6.45)
	GE-FL	62.9(1.53)				
news3	EM-FL	70.7(2.41)	70.65(2.06)	71.0(1.84)	71.08(1.63)	71.73(1.24)
	EM-FL	21.64(6.44)	29.15(6.68)	36.04(5.33)	47.75(5.38)	57.3(2.91)
	GE-FL	**75.39(2.53)**				
ohscal	EM-FL	57.19(0.84)	57.35(0.74)	57.95(0.68)	58.4(1.11)	59.22(1.06)
	EM	38.48(7.24)	46.53(5.27)	51.01(4.1)	57.34(2.26)	**59.88(2.13)**
	GE-FL	57.28(0.64)				
sraa	EM-FL	94.94(1.25)	94.98(1.23)	94.93(1.22)	94.91(1.24)	94.73(1.43)
	EM	58.02(25.38)	69.79(15.26)	79.44(12.76)	85.84(6.5)	91.43(1.52)
	GE-FL	**99.43(0.04)**				
webkb	EM-FL	86.12(0.81)	86.15(0.75)	86.09(0.8)	86.01(1.03)	**86.36(0.88)**
	EM	45.55(23.4)	42.03(16.24)	52.08(20.22)	43.16(9.07)	55.08(18.67)
	GE-FL	82.53(1.06)				

Table 2: Performance Results for varying number of labeled samples

6.2.1 Varying Unlabeled Data

Dataset	Algo	fraction of unlabeled examples used				
		0.1	0.2	0.3	0.4	0.5
20 News	EM-FL	50.01(4.85)	59.47(1.84)	**64.61(2.18)**	**67.01(1.36)**	**69.72(0.94)**
	EM	11.14(2.8)	18.55(3.67)	23.27(6.84)	27.53(2.94)	31.38(5)
	GE-FL	**56.36(1.19)**	**59.63(1.84)**	60.42(1.07)	60.94(0.52)	62.69(0.99)
SRAA	EM-FL	79.67(0.48)	82.49(0.43)	88.27(0.33)	92.05(0.71)	94.71(0.43)
	EM	58.36(2.74)	72.56(8.84)	79.44(0.34)	79.43(0.46)	79.67(0.4)
	GE-FL	**99.18(0.1)**	**99.35(0.1)**	**99.32(0.12)**	**99.37(0.04)**	**99.44(0.08)**
news3	EM-FL	41.92(1.94)	54.05(2.84)	60.98(1.13)	64.26(0.73)	67.99(1.59)
	EM	42.25(2.59)	41.06(3.21)	42.84(2.54)	45.27(2.6)	48.17(2.3)
	GE-FL	**56.1(5.52)**	**64.79(1.11)**	**68.53(1.56)**	**67.61(2.05)**	**71.02(0.81)**
ohscal	EM-FL	**62.43(2.153)**	**65.21(1.526)**	**64.98(0.957)**	**65.03(0.996)**	**62.83(2.016)**
	EM	61.54(2.14)	63.59(1.577)	63.02(1.22)	64.19(1.2)	61.48(2.039)
	GE-FL	49.284(2.91)	53.55(2.052)	54.21(1.377)	57.74(0.906)	55.5(0.568)
webkb	EM-FL	73.76(3.1)	**79(4.48)**	**81.93(1.5)**	**84.04(1.03)**	**85.17(1.49)**
	EM	73.76(8.25)	65.59(7.26)	74.95(1.28)	78.31(2.16)	74.26(3.8)
	GE-FL	**77.07(2.74)**	78.75(1.23)	81.05(1.28)	81.05(0.6)	81.05(1.5)

Table 3: Performance Results for varying fraction of unlabeled data

We have conducted a set of experiments by varying the number of unlabeled data samples from which the classifier is learnt using feature constraints. For each dataset, we vary the amount of training data from 0.1 to 0.5 in steps of 0.1, of the total amount of data. The amount of test data is fixed at 0.1 fraction of total data. The number of feature constraints are kept same as the previous experiment. We kept the number of labeled examples available for training EM-FL and EM algorithms as 512. As observed in the Table 3, EM-FL performs better than GE-FL in 3 datasets. GE-FL learns the classifier very accurately for the sraa dataset as observed before.

6.2.2 Performance

Training a GE-FL classifier from a large dataset such as news3 requires significant computation resources as it is based on global optimization requiring L-BFGS to be run on a parameter space equal to the number of features. Our approach consists of much lighter optimization where the number of parameters for L-BFGS is much smaller, hence converges faster. (Fujino et al., 2008) have given that the number of steps for convergence of their objective function is 160, under similar conditions on webkb dataset, our objective converges in 15 steps. Training GE-FL classifier on news3 dataset took 110.78 seconds (on a system with 2GHz processor and 2GB RAM) where as training a EM-FL classifier takes 42.59 seconds.

6.3 TransferLearning

Table 4: Multi Domain Sentiment Dataset for Transfer Learning

NameOfDataset	Description	No of Classes	No of Features
Books [5]	2000 instances	2 classes	473,856
DVD	2000 instances	2 classes	
Electronics	2000 instances	2 classes	
Kitchen	2000 instances	2 classes	

We use Multi Domain Sentiment analysis dataset developed by (Blitzer, 2008). This dataset contains product reviews collected at amazon. There are 4 sets of reviews, each of which contains 2000 positive/negative documents. It is already pre-processed. We make 12 transfer learning tasks of these 4 datasets. Here B–D indicates the task is to use labeled data of Books dataset and learn a classifier for the domain DVD for which there is no labeled data. We use 100 features collected through mutual information from source domain and use them as the constraints for the target domain to learn a classifier. We just use mutual information which requires one pass through the dataset. In most cases our approach is comparable to that of (Blitzer, 2008). But we observe that our results are a notch behind that of the results obtained in (Pan et al., 2010). This is because our approach does not take the benefit of co-clustering which requires building the graph of co-occurrences. We conducted another experiment varying the

	B–D	D–B	B–E	E–B	B–K	K–B	D–E	E–D	D–K	K–D	E–K	K–E
Base	0.759	0.762	0.66	0.719	0.719	0.729	0.667	0.735	0.734	0.758	0.851	0.825
GE-FL	**0.773**	0.771	0.707	**0.767**	0.775	**0.735**	0.713	**0.781**	0.737	**0.795**	0.822	0.821
SCL	0.758	**0.797**	**0.759**	0.754	**0.789**	0.686	**0.741**	0.762	**0.814**	0.767	**0.859**	**0.868**

Table 5: Transfer Learning Results

number of labeled features. We varied them from 50-250 in steps of 50. We observed that too many features is not benefiting the classification accuracy and roughly 150-200 features are enough to improve significantly from the baseline. In all our experiments we averaged over the 10 runs of the same algorithm. The results are plotted and given in figure 1.

7 Conclusion & Future Work

Though the problem of adapting naive bayes approach with discriminative constraints has been addressed previously most of them are based on working with multi-objective optimization problem, which does not have theoretical convergence properties. In the current work, we instead used an objective function which learns both from labeled data and feature constraints

[5] http://www.cs.jhu.edu/ mdredze/datasets/sentiment/

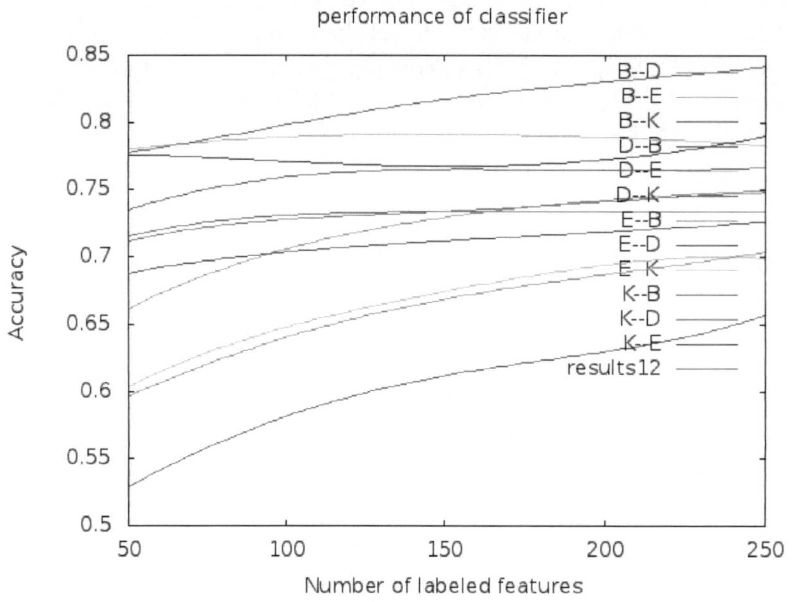

Figure 1: Performance of Feature transfer Learning

over unlabeled data and yet resulting in a single point solution. Our experimental results show how very few feature constraints (infact one cosntraint per class) can also help to improve the classifier by a significant margin over the base-line. From a computational efficiency point of view, our approach takes much lesser time compared to GE-FL as we use a combination of naive bayes and maximum entropy. It still remains an open question how to incorporate GE type of constraints in a semi-supervised setup. We have shown an application of our framework to the transfer learning problem. Empirical results show that it is competent with state of art approaches with out incurring extra computational burden.

References

Bellare, K., Druck, G., and McCallum, A. (2009). Alternating projections for learning with expectation constraints. In *UAI*, pages 43–50.

Blei, D. M., Ng, A. Y., and Jordan, M. I. (2003). Latent dirichlet allocation. *Journal of Machine Learning Research*, 3:993–1022.

Blitzer, J. (2008). *Domain Adaptation of Natural Language Processing Systems*. PhD thesis, University of Pennsylvania.

Dai, W., Xue, G.-R., Yang, Q., and Yu, Y. (2007). Transferring naive bayes classifiers for text classification. In *Proceedings of the 22nd national conference on Artificial intelligence - Volume 1*, AAAI'07, pages 540–545. AAAI Press.

Dempster, A. P., Laird, N. M., and Rubin, D. B. (1977). Maximum likelihood from incomplete data via em algorithm. *Journal of the Royal Statistical Society Series BMethodological*, 39(1):1–38.

Druck, G., Mann, G., and McCallum, A. (2008). Learning from labeled features using generalized expectation criteria. In *Proceedings of the 31st annual international ACM SIGIR conference on Research and development in information retrieval*, SIGIR '08, pages 595–602, New York, NY, USA. ACM.

Druck, G., Mann, G. S., and McCallum, A. (2009). Semi-supervised learning of dependency parsers using generalized expectation criteria. In *ACL/AFNLP*, pages 360–368.

Druck, G. and McCallum, A. (2010). High-performance semi-supervised learning using discriminatively constrained generative models. In *ICML*, pages 319–326.

Druck, G., Pal, C., McCallum, A., and Zhu, X. (2007). Semi-supervised classification with hybrid generative/discriminative methods. In *KDD*, pages 280–289.

Dudik, M. (2007). *Maximum entropy density estimation and modeling geographic distributions of species*. PhD thesis, Princeton, NJ, USA. AAI3281302.

Fujino, A., Ueda, N., and Saito, K. (2008). Semisupervised learning for a hybrid generative/discriminative classifier based on the maximum entropy principle. *IEEE Trans. Pattern Anal. Mach. Intell.*, 30(3):424–437.

Ganchev, K., Graça, J. a., Gillenwater, J., and Taskar, B. (2010). Posterior regularization for structured latent variable models. *J. Mach. Learn. Res.*, 11:2001–2049.

Graça, J., Ganchev, K., and Taskar, B. (2007). Expectation maximization and posterior constraints. In *NIPS*.

Lin, C. and He, Y. (2009). Joint sentiment/topic model for sentiment analysis. In *CIKM*, pages 375–384.

Liu, B., Li, X., Lee, W. S., and Yu, P. S. (2004). Text classification by labeling words. In *Proceedings of the 19th national conference on Artifical intelligence*, AAAI'04, pages 425–430. AAAI Press.

Mann, G. S. and McCallum, A. (2010). Generalized expectation criteria for semi-supervised learning with weakly labeled data. *Journal of Machine Learning Research*, 11:955–984.

Melville, P., Gryc, W., and Lawrence, R. D. (2009). Sentiment analysis of blogs by combining lexical knowledge with text classification. In *KDD*, pages 1275–1284.

Neal, R. M. and Hinton, G. E. (1993). A new view of the em algorithm that justifies incremental and other variants. *Learning in Graphical Models*, pages 355–368.

Ng, A. Y. and Jordan, M. I. (2002). On discriminative vs. generative classifiers: A comparison of logistic regression and naive bayes. *Advances in neural information processing systems*, 2(14):841–848.

Nigam, K. P. (2001). *Using unlabeled data to improve text classification*. PhD thesis, Pittsburgh, PA, USA. AAI3040487.

O. Chapelle, B. S. and Zien, A. (2006). *Semi-Supervised Learning*. MIT Press, Cambridge, MA,.

Pan, S. J., Ni, X., Sun, J.-T., Yang, Q., and Chen, Z. (2010). Cross-domain sentiment classification via spectral feature alignment. In *WWW*, pages 751–760.

Pan, S. J. and Yang, Q. (2010). A survey on transfer learning. *IEEE Trans. Knowl. Data Eng.*, 22(10):1345–1359.

Raina, R., Ng, A. Y., and Koller, D. (2006). Constructing informative priors using transfer learning. In *ICML*, pages 713–720.

Sindhwani, V., Hu, J., and Mojsilovic, A. (2008). Regularized co-clustering with dual supervision. In *NIPS*, pages 1505–1512.

Su, J., Shirab, J. S., and Matwin, S. (2011). Large scale text classification using semisupervised multinomial naive bayes. In *ICML*, pages 97–104.

Tan, S., Cheng, X., Wang, Y., and Xu, H. (2009). Adapting naive bayes to domain adaptation for sentiment analysis. In *Proceedings of the 31th European Conference on IR Research on Advances in Information Retrieval*, ECIR '09, pages 337–349, Berlin, Heidelberg. Springer-Verlag.

Optimization and Sampling for NLP from a Unified Viewpoint

Marc DYMETMAN[1] Guillaume BOUCHARD[1] Simon CARTER[2]

(1) Xerox Research Centre Europe, Grenoble, France
(2) ISLA, University of Amsterdam, The Netherlands
{marc.dymetman,guillaume.bouchard}@xrce.xerox.com; s.c.carter@uva.nl

Abstract

The OS* algorithm is a unified approach to exact optimization and sampling, based on incremental refinements of a functional upper bound, which combines ideas of adaptive rejection sampling and of A* optimization search. We first give a detailed description of OS*. We then explain how it can be applied to several NLP tasks, giving more details on two such applications: (i) decoding and sampling with a high-order HMM, and (ii) decoding and sampling with the intersection of a PCFG and a high-order LM.

1 Introduction

Optimization and Sampling are usually seen as two completely separate tasks. However, in NLP and many other domains, the primary objects of interest are often probability distributions over discrete or continuous spaces, for which both aspects are natural: in optimization, we are looking for the mode of the distribution, in sampling we would like to produce a statistically representative set of objects from the distribution. The OS* algorithm approaches the two aspects from a unified viewpoint; it is a joint exact Optimization and Sampling algorithm that is inspired both by rejection sampling and by classical A* optimization (O S *).

Common algorithms for sampling high-dimensional distributions are based on MCMC techniques [Andrieu et al., 2003, Robert and Casella, 2004], which are approximate in the sense that they produce valid samples only asymptotically. By contrast, the elementary technique of Rejection Sampling [Robert and Casella, 2004] directly produces exact samples, but, if applied naively to high-dimensional spaces, typically requires unacceptable time before producing a first sample.

By contrast, OS* can be applied to high-dimensional spaces. The main idea is to upper-bound the complex target distribution p by a simpler proposal distribution q, such that a dynamic programming (or another low-complexity) method can be applied to q in order to efficiently sample or maximize from it. In the case of sampling, rejection sampling is then applied to q, and on a reject at point x, q is refined into a slightly more complex q' in an adaptive way. This is done by using the evidence of the reject at x, which implies a gap between $q(x)$ and $p(x)$, to identify a (soft) constraint implicit in p which is not accounted for by q. This constraint is then integrated into q to obtain q'.

The constraint which is integrated tends to be highly relevant and to increase the acceptance rate of the algorithm. By contrast, many constraints that are constitutive of p are never "activated" by sampling from q, because q never explores regions where they would become visible. For example, anticipating our HMM experiments in section 3.1, there is little point in explicitly including in q a 5-gram constraint on a certain latent sequence in the HMM if this sequence

Proceedings of the First International Workshop on Optimization Techniques for Human Language Technology, pages 79–94,
COLING 2012, Mumbai, December 2012.

is already unlikely at the bigram level: the bigram constraints present in the proposal q will ensure that this sequence will never (or very rarely) be explored by q.

The case of optimization is treated in exactly the same way as sampling. Formally, this consists in moving from assessing proposals in terms of the L_1 norm to assessing them in terms of the L_∞ norm. Typically, when a dynamic programming procedure is available for sampling (L_1 norm) with q, it is also available for maximizing from q (L_∞ norm), and the main difference between the two cases is then in the criteria for selecting among possible refinements.

Related work In order to improve the acceptance rate of rejection sampling, one has to lower the proposal q curve as much as possible while keeping it above the p curve. In order to do that, some authors [Gilks and Wild, 1992, Görür and Teh, 2008], have proposed *Adaptive Rejection Sampling (ARS)* where, based on rejections, the q curve is updated to a lower curve q' with a better acceptance rate. These techniques have predominantly been applied to continuous distributions on the one-dimensional real line, where convexity assumptions on the target distribution can be exploited to progressively approximate it tighter and tighter through upper bounds consisting of piecewise linear envelopes. These sampling techniques have not been connected to optimization.

One can find a larger amount of related work in the optimization domain. In an heuristic optimization context the two interesting, but apparently little known, papers [Kam and Kopec, 1996, Popat et al., 2000], discuss a technique for decoding images based on high-order language models where upper-bounds are constructed in terms of simpler variable-order models. Our application of OS* in section 3.1 to the problem of maximizing a high-order HMM is similar to their (also exact) technique; while this work seems to be the closest to ours, the authors do not attempt to generalize their approach to other optimization problems amenable to dynamic programming. Among NLP applications, [Kaji et al., 2010, Huang et al., 2012] are another recent approach to exact optimization for sequence labelling that also has connections to our experiments in section 3.1, but differs in particular by using a less flexible refinement scheme than our variable-order n-grams. In the NLP community again, there is currently a lot of interest for optimization methods that fall in the general category of "coarse-to-fine" techniques [Petrov, 2009], which tries to guide the inference process towards promising regions that get incrementally tighter and tighter. While most of this line of research concentrates on approximate optimization, some related approaches aim at finding an exact optimum. Thus, [Tromble and Eisner, 2006] attempt to maximize a certain objective while respecting complex hard constraints, which they do by incrementally adding those constraints that are violated by the current optimum, using finite-state techniques. [Riedel and Clarke, 2006] have a similar goal, but address it by incrementally adding ILP (Integer Linear Programming) constraints. Linear Programming techniques are also involved in the recent applications of Dual Decomposition to NLP [Rush et al., 2010, Rush and Collins, 2011], which can be applied to difficult combinations of easy problems, and often are able to find an exact optimum. None of these optimization papers, to our knowledge, attempts to extend these techniques to sampling, in contrast to what we do.

Paper organization The remainder of this paper is structured as follows. In section 2, we describe the OS* algorithm, explain how it can be used for exact optimization and sampling, and show its connection to A*. In section 3, we first describe several NLP applications of the algorithm, then give more details on two such applications. The first one is an application to optimization/sampling with high-order HMMs, where we also provide experimental results; the second one is a high-level description of its application to the generic problem of optimization/sampling with the intersection of a PCFG with a high-order language model, a problem which has recently attracted some attention in the community. We finally conclude and indicate some perspectives.

2 The OS* algorithm

OS* is a unified algorithm for optimization and sampling. For simplicity, we first present its sampling version, then move to its optimization version, and finally get to the unified view. We start with some background and notations about rejection sampling.

Note: The OS approach was previously described in an e-print [Dymetman et al., 2012], where some applications beyond NLP are also provided.*

2.1 Background

Let $p : X \to \mathbb{R}_+$ be a measurable L_1 function with respect to a base measure μ on a space X, i.e. $\int_X p(x)d\mu(x) < \infty$. We define $\bar{p}(x) \equiv \frac{p(x)}{\int_X p(x)d\mu(x)}$. The function p can be seen as an unnormalized density over X, and $\bar{p}$ as a normalized density which defines a probability distribution over X, called the *target distribution*, from which we want to sample from[1]. While we may not be able to sample directly from the target distribution $\bar{p}$, let us assume that we can easily compute $p(x)$ for any given x. *Rejection Sampling* (RS) [Robert and Casella, 2004] then works as follows. We define a certain unnormalized *proposal density* q over X, which is such that (i) we know how to directly sample from it (more precisely, from $\bar{q}$), and (ii) q dominates p, i.e. for all $x \in X, p(x) \leq q(x)$. We then repeat the following process: (1) we draw a sample x from q, (2) we compute the ratio $r(x) \equiv p(x)/q(x) \leq 1$, (3) with probability $r(x)$ we accept x, otherwise we reject it, (4) we repeat the process with a new x. It can then be shown that this procedure produces an exact sample from p. Furthermore, the average rate at which it produces these samples, the *acceptance rate*, is equal to $P(X)/Q(X)$ [Robert and Casella, 2004], where for a (measurable) subset A of X, we define $P(A) \equiv \int_A p(x)d\mu(x)$ and $Q(A) \equiv \int_A q(x)d\mu(x)$. In Fig. 1, panel (S1), the acceptance rate is equal to the ratio of the area below the p curve with that below the q curve.

2.2 Sampling with OS*

The way OS* does sampling is illustrated on the top of Fig. 1. In this illustration, we start sampling with an initial proposal density q (see (S1)). Our first attempt produces x_1, for which the ratio $r_q(x_1) = p(x_1)/q(x_1)$ is close to 1; this leads, say, to the acceptance of x_1. Our second attempt produces x_2, for which the ratio $r_q(x_2) = p(x_2)/q(x_2)$ is much lower than 1, leading, say, to a rejection. Although we have a rejection, we have gained some useful information, namely that $p(x_2)$ is much lower than $q(x_2)$, and we are going to use that "evidence" to define a new proposal q' (see (S2)), which has the following properties:

- $p(x) \leq q'(x) \leq q(x)$ everywhere on X;
- $q'(x_2) < q(x_2)$.

One extreme way of obtaining such a q' is to take $q'(x)$ equal to $p(x)$ for $x = x_2$ and to $q(x)$ for $x \neq x_2$, which, when the space X is discrete, has the effect of improving the acceptance rate, but only slightly so, by insuring that any time q' happens to select x_2, it will accept it.

[1] By abuse of language, we will also say that a sample from $\bar{p}$ is a sample from p.

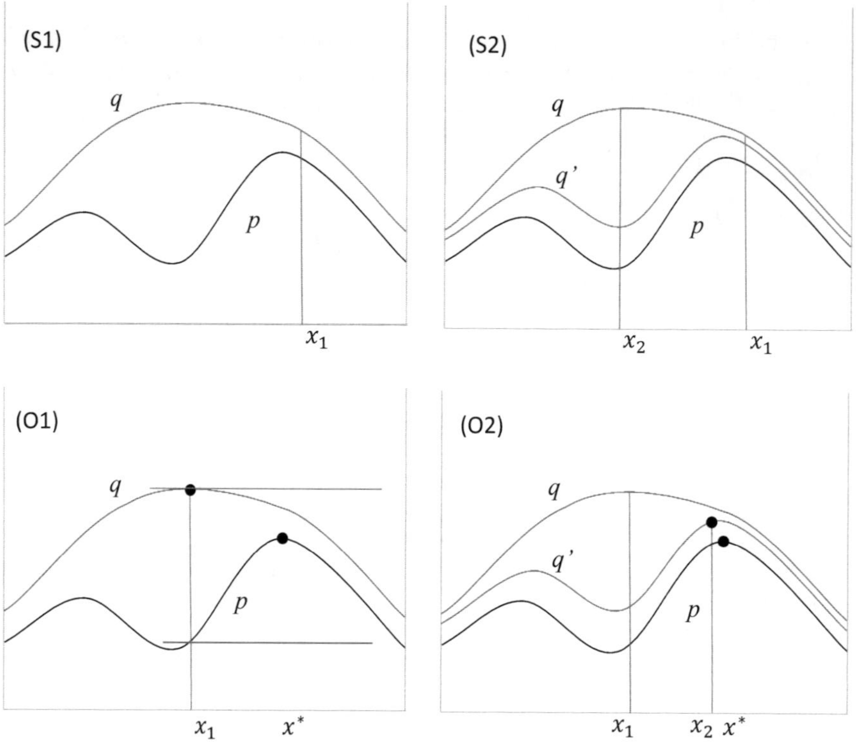

Figure 1: Sampling with OS* (S1, S2), and optimization with OS* (O1, O2).

A better generic way to find a q' is the following. Suppose that we are provided with a small finite set of "one-step refinement actions" a_j, depending on q and x_2, which are able to move from q to a new $q'_j = a_j(q, x_2)$ such that for any such a_j one has $p(x) \leq q'_j(x) \leq q(x)$ everywhere on X and also $q'_j(x_2) < q(x_2)$. Then we will select among these a_j moves the one that is such that the L_1 norm of q'_j is minimal among the possible j's, or in other words, such that $\int_X q'_j(x)d\mu(x)$ is minimal in j. The idea is that, by doing so, we will improve the acceptance rate of q'_j (which depends directly on $||q'_j||_1$) as much as possible, while (i) not having to explore a too large space of possible refinements, and (ii) moving to a representation of q'_j that is only slightly more complex than q, rather than to a much more complex representation for a q' that could result from exploring a larger space of possible refinements for q.[2] The intuition behind such one-step refinement actions a_j will become clearer when we consider concrete examples below.

2.3 Optimization with OS*

The optimization version of OS* is illustrated on the bottom of Fig. 1, where (O1) shows on the one hand the function p that we are trying to maximize from, along with its (unknown) maximum p^*, indicated by a black circle on the p curve, and corresponding to x^* in X. It also shows a "proposal" function q which is such — analogously to the sampling case — that (1) the

[2]In particular, even if we could find a refinement q' that would exactly coincide with p, and therefore would have the smallest possible L_1 norm, we might not want to use such a refinement if this involved an overly complex representation for q'.

function q is above p on the whole of the space X and (2) it is easy to directly find the point x_1 in X at which it reaches its maximum q^*, shown as a black circle on the q curve.

A simple, but central, observation is the following one. Suppose that the distance between $q(x_1)$ and $p(x_1)$ is smaller than ϵ, then the distance between $q(x_1)$ and p^* is also smaller than ϵ. This can be checked immediately on the figure, and is due to the fact that on the one hand p^* is higher than $p(x_1)$, and that on the other hand it is below $q(x^*)$, and *a fortiori* below $q(x_1)$. In other words, if the maximum that we have found for q is at a coordinate x_1 and we observe that $q(x_1) - p(x_1) < \epsilon$, then we can conclude that we have found the maximum of p up to ϵ.

In the case of x_1 in the figure, we are still far from the maximum, and so we "reject" x_1, and refine q into q' (see (O2)), using exactly the same approach as in the sampling case, but for one difference: the one-step refinement option a_j that is selected is now chosen on the basis of how much it decreases, not the L_1 norm of q, but the max of q — where, as a reminder, this max can also be notated $||q||_\infty$, using the L_∞ norm notation.[3]

Once this q' has been selected, one can then find its maximum at x_2 and then the process can be repeated with $q_1 = q, q_2 = q', \ldots$ until the difference between $q_k(x_k)$ and $p(x_k)$ is smaller than a certain predefined threshold.

2.4 Sampling L_1 vs. Optimization L_∞

While sampling and optimization are usually seen as two completely distinct tasks, they can actually be viewed as two extremities of a continuous range, when considered in the context of L_p spaces.

If (X, μ) is a measure space, and if f is a real-valued function on this space, one defines the L_p norm $||f||_p$, for $1 \leq p < \infty$ as: $||f||_p \equiv \left(\int_X |f|^p(x) d\mu(x)\right)^{1/p}$ [Rudin, 1987]. One also defines the L_∞ norm $||f||_\infty$ as: $||f||_\infty \equiv \inf\{C \geq 0 : |f(x)| \leq C \text{ for almost every } x\}$, where the right term is called the *essential supremum* of $|f|$, and can be thought of roughly as the "max" of the function. So, with some abuse of language, we can simply write: $||f||_\infty \equiv \max_{x \in X} |f|$. The space L_p, for $1 \leq p \leq \infty$, is then defined as being the space of all functions f for which $||f||_p < \infty$. Under the simple condition that $||f||_p < \infty$ for some $p < \infty$, we have: $\lim_{p \to \infty} ||f||_p = ||f||_\infty$.

The standard notion of sampling is relative to L_1. However we can introduce the following generalization — where we use the notation L_α instead of L_p in order to avoid confusion with our use of p for denoting the target distribution. We will say that we are performing *sampling of a non-negative function f relative to $L_\alpha(X, \mu)$*, for $1 \leq \alpha < \infty$, if $f \in L_\alpha(X, \mu)$ and if we sample — in the standard sense — according to the normalized density distribution $\bar{f}(x) \equiv \frac{f(x)^\alpha}{\int_X f(x)^\alpha d\mu(x)}$. In the case $\alpha = \infty$, we will say that we are sampling relative to $L_\infty(X, \mu)$, if $f \in L_\infty(X, \mu)$ and if we are performing optimization relative to f, more precisely, if for any $\epsilon > 0$, we are able to find an x such that $|||f||_\infty - f(x)| < \epsilon$.

Informally, sampling relative to L_α "tends" to sampling with L_∞ (i.e. optimization), for α tending to ∞, in the sense that for a large α, an x sampled relative to L_α "tends" to be close to a maximum for f. We will not attempt to give a precise formal meaning to that observation here, but just note the connection with the idea of *simulated annealing* [Kirkpatrick et al.,

[3] A formal definition of that norm is that $||q||_\infty$ is equal to the "essential supremum" of q over (X, μ) (see below), but for all practical purposes here, it is enough to think of this essential supremum as being the max, when it exists.

1983], which we can view as a mix between the MCMC Metropolis-Hastings sampling technique [Robert and Casella, 2004] and the idea of sampling in L_α spaces with larger and larger α's.

In summary, we thus can view optimization as an extreme form of sampling. In the sequel we will often use this generalized sense of sampling in our algorithms.[4]

2.5 OS* as a unified algorithm

The general design of OS* can be described as follows:

- Our goal is to OS-sample from p, where we take the expression "OS-sample" to refer to a generalized sense that covers both sampling (in the standard sense) and optimization.

- We have at our disposal a family $\mathcal{Q}$ of proposal densities over the space (X, μ), such that, for every $q \in \mathcal{Q}$, we are able to OS-sample efficiently from q.

- Given a reject x_1 relative to a proposal q, with $p(x_1) < q(x_1)$, we have at our disposal a (limited) number of possible "one-step" refinement options q', with $p \leq q' \leq q$, and such that $q'(x_1) < q(x_1)$.

- We then select one such q'. One possible selection criterion is to prefer the q' which has the smallest L_1 norm (sampling case) or L_∞ norm (optimization). In one sense, this is the most natural criterion, as it means we are directly lowering the norm that controls the efficiency of the OS-sampling. For instance, for sampling, if q'_1 and q'_2 are two candidates refinements with $||q'_1||_1 < ||q'_2||_1$, then the acceptance rate of q'_1 is larger than that of q'_2, simply because then $P(X)/Q'_1(X) > P(X)/Q'_2(X)$. Similarly, in optimization, if $||q'_1||_\infty < ||q'_2||_\infty$, then the gap between $\max_x(q'_1(x))$ and p^* is smaller than that between $\max_x(q'_2(x))$ and p^*, simply because then $\max_x(q'_1(x)) < \max_x(q'_2(x))$. However, using this criterion may require the computation of the norm of each of the possible one-step refinements, which can be costly, and one can prefer simpler criteria, for instance simply selecting the q' that minimizes $q'(x_1)$.

- We iterate until we settle on a "good" q: either (in sampling) one which is such that the cumulative acceptance rate until this point is above a certain threshold; or (in optimization) one for which the ratio $p(x_1)/q(x_1)$ is closer to 1 than a certain threshold, with x_1 being the maximum for q.

The following algorithm gives a unified view of OS*, valid for both sampling and optimization. This is a high-level view, with some of the content delegated to the subroutines `OS-Sample`, `Accept-or-Reject`, `Update`, `Refine`, `Stop`, which are described in the text.

[4]Note: While our two experiments in section ?? are based on discrete spaces, the OS* algorithm is more general, and *can be applied to any measurable space (in particular continuous spaces)*; in such cases, p and q have to be measurable functions, and the relation $p \leq q$ should be read as $p(x) \leq q(x)$ a.e. (almost everywhere) relative to the base measure μ.

Algorithm 1 The OS* algorithm

1: **while not** Stop(h) **do**
2: OS-Sample $x \sim q$
3: $r \leftarrow p(x)/q(x)$
4: Accept-or-Reject(x, r)
5: Update(h, x)
6: **if** Rejected(x) **then**
7: $q \leftarrow$ Refine(q, x)
8: **return** q along with accepted x's in h

On entry into the algorithm, we assume that we are either in sample mode or in optimization mode, and also that we are starting from a proposal q which (1) dominates p and (2) from which we can sample or optimize directly. We use the terminology *OS-Sample* to represent either of these cases, where `OS-Sample` $x \sim q$ refers to sampling an x according to the proposal q or optimizing x on q (namely finding an x which is an argmax of q, a common operation for many NLP tasks), depending on the case. On line (1), h refers to the history of the sampling so far, namely to the set of trials $x_1, x_2, ...$ that have been done so far, each being marked for acceptance or rejection (in the case of sampling, this is the usual notion, in the case of optimization, all but the last proposal will be marked as rejects). The stopping criterion `Stop(`h`)` will be to stop: (i) *in sampling mode*, if the number of acceptances so far relative to the number of trials is larger than a certain predefined threshold, and in this case will return on line (8), first, the list of accepted x's so far, which is already a valid sample from p, and second, the last refinement q, which can then be used to produce any number of future samples as desired with an acceptance ratio similar to the one observed so far; (ii) *in optimization mode*, if the last element x of the history is an accept, and in this case will return on line (8), first the value x, which in this mode is the only accepted trial in the history, and second, the last refinement q (which can be used for such purposes as providing a "certificate of optimality of x relative to p", but we do not detail this here).

On line (3), we compute the ratio r, and then on line (4) we decide to accept x or not based on this ratio; in optimization mode, we accept x if the ratio is close enough to 1, as determined by a threshold[5]; in sampling mode, we accept x based on a Bernoulli trial of probability r.

On line (5), we update the history by recording the trial x and whether it was accepted or not.

If x was rejected (line (6)), then on line (7), we perform a refinement of q, based on the principles that we have explained.

2.6 A connection with A*

A special case of the OS* algorithm, which we call "OS* with piecewise bounds", shows a deep connection with the classical A* optimization algorithm [Hart et al., 1968] and is interesting in its own right. Let us first focus on sampling, and suppose that q_0 represents an initial proposal density, which upper-bounds the target density p over X. We start by sampling with q_0, and on a first reject somewhere in X, we split the set X into two disjoint subsets X_1, X_2, obtaining a partition of X. By using the more precise context provided by this partition, we may be able

[5] When X is a finite domain, it makes sense to stop on a ratio *equal* to 1, in which case we have found an exact maximum. This is what we do in our experiments in section 3.1.

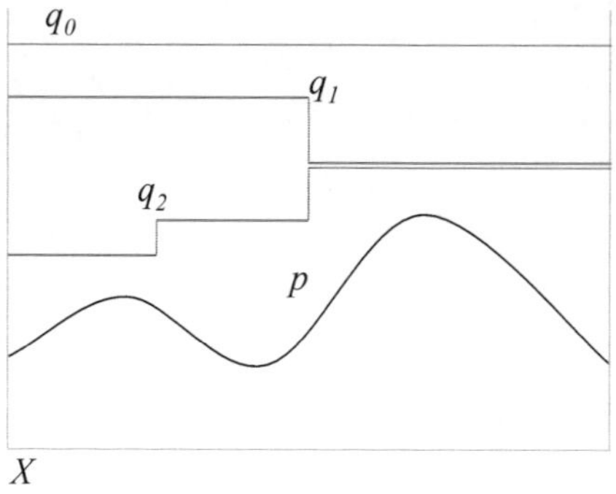

Figure 2: A connection with A*.

to improve our upper bound q_0 over the whole of X into tighter upper bounds on each of X_1 and X_2, resulting then in a new upper bound q_1 over the whole of X. We then sample using q_1, and experience at some later time another reject, say on a point in X_1; at this point we again partition X_1 into two subsets X_{11} and X_{12}, tighten the bounds on these subsets, and obtain a refined proposal q_2 over X; we then iterate the process of building this "hierarchical partition" until we reach a certain acceptance-rate threshold.

If we now move our focus to optimization, we see that the refinements that we have just proposed present an analogy to the technique used by A*. This is illustrated in Fig. 2. In A*, we start with a *constant* optimistic bound — corresponding to our q_0 — for the objective function which is computed at the root of the search tree, which we can assume to be binary. We then expand the two daughters of the root, re-evaluate the optimistic bounds there to new constants, obtaining the piecewise constant proposal q_1, and move to the daughter with the highest bound. We continue by expanding at each step the leaf of the partial search tree with the highest optimistic bound (e.g. moving from q_1 to q_2, etc.).

It is important to note that OS*, when used in optimization mode, is in fact *strictly more general than A**, for two reasons: (i) it does not assume a piecewise refinement strategy, namely that the refinements follow a hierarchical partition of the space, where a given refinement is limited to a leaf of the current partition, and (ii) even if such a stategy is followed, it does not assume that the piecewise upper-bounds are constant. Both points will become clearer in the HMM experiments of section 3.1, where including an higher-order n-gram in q has impact on several regions of X simultaneously, possibly overlapping in complex ways with regions touched by previous refinements; in addition, the impact of a single n-gram is non-constant even in the regions it touches, because it depends of the multiplicity of the n-gram, not only on its presence or absence.

3 Some NLP applications of OS*

The OS* framework appears to have many applications to NLP problems where we need to optimize or sample from a complex objective function p. Let us give a partial list of such situations:

- Efficient decoding and sampling with high-order HMM's.
- Combination of a probabilistic context free grammar (PCFG) with a complex finite-state automaton (FSA):

- Tagging by joint usage of a PCFG and a HMM tagger;
- Hierarchical translation with a complex target language model

- Parsing in the presence of non-local features.
- PCFG's with transversal constraints, probabilistic unification grammars.

We will not explore all of these situations here, but will concentrate on (i) decoding and sampling with high-order HMM's, for which we provide details and experimental results, and (ii) combining a PCFG with a complex finite-state language model, which we only describe at a high-level. We hope these two illustrations will suffice to give a feeling of the power of the technique.

3.1 High-Order HMMs

Note: An extended and much more detailed version of these HMM experiments is provided in [Carter et al., 2012].

The objective in our HMM experiments is to sample a word sequence with density $\bar{p}(x)$ proportional to $p(x) = p_{\text{lm}}(x)\ p_{\text{obs}}(o|x)$, where p_{lm} is the probability of the sequence x under an n-gram model and $p_{\text{obs}}(o|x)$ is the probability of observing the noisy sequence of observations o given that the word sequence is x. Assuming that the observations depend only on the current state, this probability can be written:

$$p(x) \quad = \quad \prod_{i=1}^{\ell} p_{\text{lm}}(x_i|x_{i-n+1}^{i-1})\ p_{\text{obs}}(o_i|x_i)\ . \tag{1}$$

Approach Taking a tri-gram language model for simplicity, let us define $w_3(x_i|x_{i-2}x_{i-1}) = p_{\text{lm}}(x_i|x_{i-2}x_{i-1})\ p_{\text{obs}}(o_i|x_i)$. Then consider the observation o be fixed, and write $p(x) = \prod_i w_3(x_i|x_{i-2}x_{i-1})$. In optimization/decoding, we want to find the argmax of $p(x)$, and in sampling, to sample from $p(x)$. Note that the state space associated with p can be huge, as we need to represent explicitly all contexts (x_{i-2}, x_{i-1}) in the case of a trigram model, and even more contexts for higher-order models.

We define $w_2(x_i|x_{i-1}) = \max_{x_{i-2}} w_3(x_i|x_{i-2}x_{i-1})$, along with $w_1(x_i) = \max_{x_{i-1}} w_2(x_i|x_{i-1})$, where the maxima are taken over all possible context words in the vocabulary. These quantities, which can be precomputed efficiently, can be seen as optimistic "max-backoffs" of the trigram x_{i-2}^{i}, where we have forgotten some part of the context. Our initial proposal is then $q_0(x) = \prod_i w_1(x_i)$. Clearly, for any sequence x of words, we have $p(x) \leq q_0(x)$. The state space of q_0 is much less costly to represent than that of $p(x)$.

The proposals q_t, which incorporate n-grams of variable orders, can be represented efficiently through weighted FSAs (WFSAs). In Fig. 3(a), we show a WFSA representing the initial proposal q_0 corresponding to an example with four observations, which we take to be the acoustic realizations of the words 'the, two, dogs, barked'. The weights on edges correspond only to unigram max-backoffs, and thus each state corresponds to a NULL-context. Over this WFSA, both optimization and sampling can be done efficiently by the standard dynamic programming techniques (Viterbi [Rabiner, 1989] and "backward filtering-forward sampling" [Scott, 2002]), where the forward weights associated to states are computed similarly, either in the max-product or in the sum-product semiring.

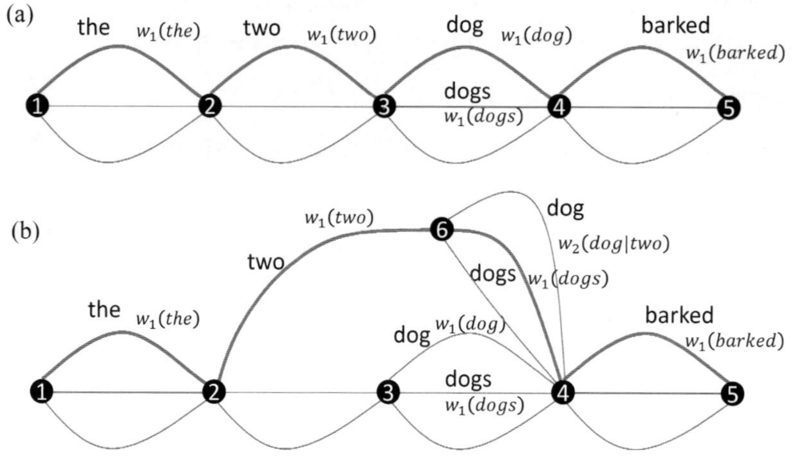

Figure 3: *An example of an initial q-automaton (a), and its refinement (b).*

Consider first sampling, and suppose that the first sample from q_0 produces $x_1 =$ *the two dog barked*, marked with bold edges in the drawing. Now, computing the ratio $p(x_1)/q_0(x_1)$ gives a result much smaller than 1, in part because from the viewpoint of the full model p, the trigram *the two dog* is very unlikely; i.e. the ratio $w_3(dog|the\ two)/w_1(dog)$ is very low. Thus, with high probability, x_1 is rejected. When this is the case, we produce a refined proposal q_1, represented by the WFSA in Fig. 3(b), which takes into account the more realistic bigram weight $w_2(dog|two)$ by adding a node (node 6) for the context *two*. We then perform a sampling trial with q_1, which this time tends to avoid producing *dog* in the context of *two*; if we experience a reject later on some sequence x_2, we refine again, meaning that we identify an n-gram in x_2, which, if we extend its context by one (e.g from a unigram to a bigram or from a bigram to a trigram), accounts for some significant part of the gap between $q_1(x_2)$ and $p(x_2)$. We stop the refinement process when we start observing acceptance rates above a certain fixed threshold.

The case of optimization is similar. Suppose that with q_0 the maximum is $x_1 =$ *the two dog barked*, then we observe that $p(x_1)$ is lower than $q_0(x_1)$, reject x_1 and refine q_0 into q_1. We stop the process at the point where the value of q_t, at its maximum x_{q_t}, is equal to the value of p at x_{q_t}, which implies that we have found the maximum for p.

Setup We evaluate our approach on an SMS-message retrieval task. Let N be the number of possible words in the vocabulary. A latent variable $x \in \{1, \cdots, N\}^\ell$ represents a sentence defined as a sequence of ℓ words. Each word is converted into a sequence of numbers based on a mobile phone numeric keypad, assuming some level of random noise in the conversion. The task is then to recover the original message.

We use the English side of the Europarl corpus [Koehn, 2005] for training and test data (1.3 million sentences). A 5-gram language model is trained using SRILM [Stolcke, 2002] on 90% of the sentences. On the remaining 10%, we randomly select 100 sequences for lengths 1 to 10 to obtain 1000 sequences from which we remove the ones containing numbers, obtaining a test set of size 926.

Optimization We limit the average number of latent tokens in our decoding experiments to 1000. In the plot (d1) of Fig. 4 we show the average number of iterations (running Viterbi then

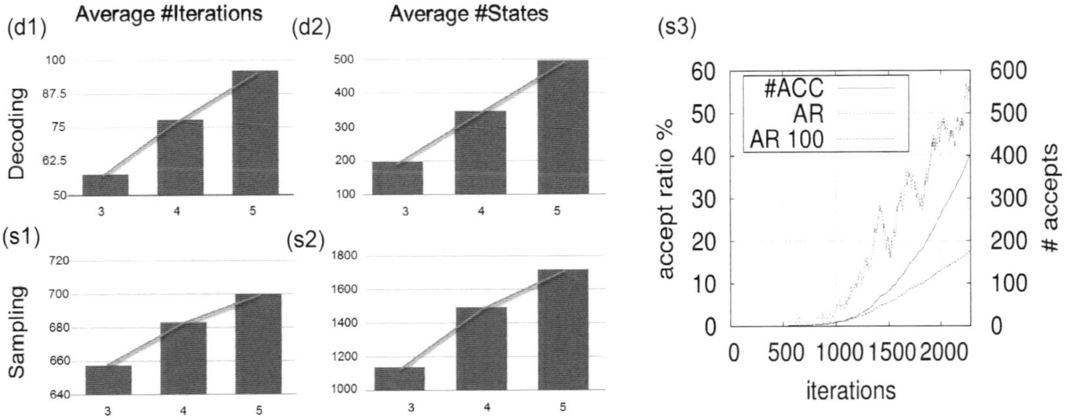

Figure 4: SMS experiments.

updating q) that the different n-gram models of size 3, 4 and 5 take to do exact decoding of the sentences of fixed length (10 words) in the test-set. We can see that decoding with larger n-gram models tends to show a linear increase w.r.t. n in the number of iterations taken. Plot (d2) shows the average number of states in the final automaton q for the same sentences, also showing a linear increase with n (rather than the exponential growth expected if all the possible states were represented). We also display in Table 1 the distribution of n-grams in the final model for one specific sentence of length 10. Note that the total number of n-grams in the full model would be $\sim 3.0 \times 10^{15}$; exact decoding here is not tractable using existing techniques. By comparison, our HMM has only 118 five-grams and 9008 n-grams in total.

n:	1	2	3	4	5
q:	7868	615	231	176	118

Table 1: *# of n-grams in our variable-order HMM.*

Sampling For the sampling experiments, we limit the number of latent tokens to 100. We refine our q automaton until we reach a certain fixed cumulative acceptance rate (AR). We also compute a rate based only on the last 100 trials (AR-100), as this tends to better reflect the current acceptance rate. In plot (s3) of Fig. 4, we show a single sampling run using a 5-gram model for an example input, and the cumulative # of accepts (middle curve). It took 500 iterations before the first successful sample from p.

We noted that there is a trade-off between the time needed to compute the forward probability weights needed for sampling, and the time it takes to adapt the variable-order HMM. To resolve this, we use batch-updates: making B trials from the same q-automaton, and then updating our model in one step. By doing this, we noted significant speed-ups in sampling times. Empirically, we found $B = 100$ to be a good value, leading to an order of magnitude improvement in speed. In plots (s1) and (s2), we show the average # of iterations and states in our models until refinements are finished (for an AR-100 of 20%), for different orders n over sentences of length 10 in the test set. We note linear trends in the number of iterations and states when moving to higher n; for length=10, and for $n = 3,4,5$, average number of iterations: 3-658, 4-683, 5-701; averager number of states: 3-1139, 4-1494, 5-1718. In particular the number of states is again much lower than the exponential increase we would expect if using the full underlying state space.

3.2 OS* for intersecting PCFG's with high-order LM's

We now move to a high-level description of the application of OS* to an important class of problems (including hierarchical SMT) which involve the intersection of PCFG's with high-order language models. The study of similar "agreement-based" problems involving optimization (but not sampling) over a combination of two individual tasks have recently been the focus of a lot of attention in the NLP community, in particular with the application of dual decomposition methods [Rush et al., 2010, Rush and Collins, 2011, Chang and Collins, 2011]. We only sketch the main ideas of our approach.

A standard result of formal language theory is that the intersection of a CFG with a FSA is a CFG [Bar-Hillel et al., 1961]. This construct can be generalized to the intersection of a Weighted CFG (WCFG) with a WFSA (see e.g. [Nederhof and Satta, 2003]), resulting in a WCFG. In our case, we will be interested in optimizing and sampling from the intersection p of a PCFG[6] G with a complex WFSA A representing a high-order language model. For illustration purposes here, we will suppose that A is a trigram language model, but the description can be easily transposed to higher-order cases.

Let us denote by x a derivation in G, and by $y = y(x)$ the string of terminal leaves associated with x (the "yield" of the derivation x). The weighted intersection p of G and A is defined as: $p(x) \equiv G(x).A(x)$, where $A(x)$ is a shorthand for $A(y(x))$.

Due to the intersection result, p can in principle be represented by a WCFG, but for a trigram model A, this grammar can become very large. Our approach will then be the following: we will start by taking the proposal $q^{(0)}$ equal to G, and then gradually refine this proposal by incorporating more and more accurate approximations to the full automaton A, themselves expressed as weighted automata of small complexity. We will stop refining based on having found a good enough approximation in optimization, or a sampler with sufficient acceptance rate in sampling.

To be precise, let us consider a PCFG G, with $\sum_x G(x) = 1$, where x varies among all the finite derivations relative to G.[7] Let us first note that it is very simple to sample from G: just expand derivations top-down using the conditional probabilities of the rules. It is also very easy to find the derivation x of maximum value $G(x)$ by a standard dynamic programming procedure.

We are going to introduce a sequence of proposals $q^{(0)} = G, q^{(1)} = q^{(0)}.B^{(1)}, ..., q^{(i+1)} = q^{(i)}.B^{(i+1)}, ...$, where each $B^{(i)}$ is a small automaton including some additional knowledge about the language model represented by A. Each $q^{(i)}$ will thus be a WCFG (not normalized) and refining $q^{(i)}$ into $q^{(i+1)}$ will then consist of a "local" update of the grammar $q^{(i)}$, ensuring a desirable incrementality of the refinements.

Analogous to the HMM case, we define: $w_3(x_5|x_3x_4) = \max_{x_2} w_4(x_5|x_2x_3x_4)$, $w_2(x_5|x_4) = \max_{x_3} w_4(x_5|x_3x_4)$, and $w_1(x_5) = \max_{x_4} w_4(x_5|x_4)$.

[6]A Probabilistic CFG (PCFG) is a special case of a WCFG.

[7]Such a PCFG is said to be consistent, that is, it is such that the total mass of infinite derivations is null [Wetherell, 1980]. We do not go into the details of this (standard) assumption here.

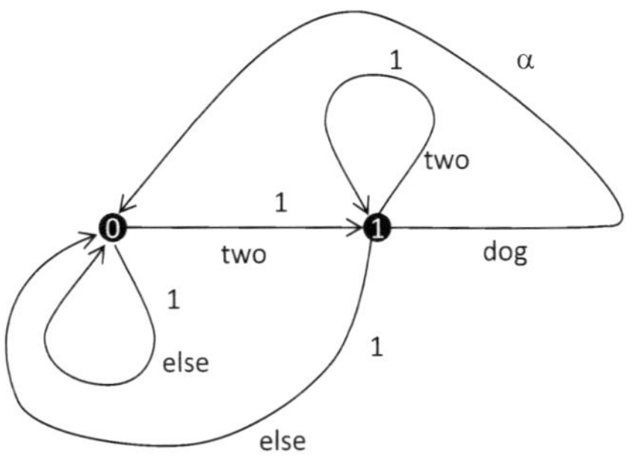

Figure 5: The "TwoDog" automaton.

Let's first consider the optimization case, and suppose that, at a certain stage, the grammar $q^{(i)}$ has already "incorporated" knowledge of $w_1(dog)$. Then suppose that the maximum derivation $x^{(i)} = \text{argmax}^{(i)}(x)$ has the yield: *the two dog barked*, where $w_1(dog)$ is much larger than the more accurate $w_2(dog|two)$.

We then decide to update $q^{(i)}$ into $q^{(i+1)} = q^{(i)}.B^{(i+1)}$, where $B^{(i+1)}$ represents the additional knowledge corresponding to $w_2(dog|two)$. More precisely, let us define:

$$\alpha \equiv \frac{w_2(dog|two)}{w_1(dog)}.$$

Clearly $\alpha \leq 1$ by the definition of w_1, w_2. Now consider the following two-state automaton $B^{(i+1)}$, which we will call the "TwoDog" automaton:

In this automaton, the state (0) is both initial and final, and (1) is only final. The state (1) can be interpreted as meaning "I have just produced the word *two*". All edges carry a weight of 1, apart from the edge labelled *dog*, which carries a weight of α. The "else" label on the arrow from (0) to itself is a shorthand that means: "any word other than *two*", and the "else" label on the arrow from (1) to (0) has the meaning: "any word other than *dog* or *two*".

It can be checked that this automaton has the following behavior: it gives a word sequence the weight α^k, where k is the number of times the sequence contains the subsequence *two dog*.

Thus, when intersected with the grammar $q^{(i)}$, this automaton produces the grammar $q^{(i+1)}$, which is such that $q^{(i+1)}(x) = q^{(i)}(x)$ if the yield of x does not contain the subsequence *two dog*, but such that $q^{(i+1)}(x) = \alpha^k.q^{(i)}(x)$ if it contains this subsequence k times. Note that because $q^{(i)}$ had already "recorded" the knowledge about $w_1(dog)$, it now assigns to the word *dog* in the context of *two* the weight $w_2(dog|two) = w_1(dog).\alpha$, while it still assigns to it in all other contexts the weight $w_1(dog)$, as desired.[8]

We will not go here into the detailed mechanics of intersecting the automaton "TwoDog" with the WCFG $q^{(i)}$, (see [Nederhof and Satta, 2008] for one technique), but just note that, because this automaton only contains two states and only one edge whose weight is not 1, this intersection can be carried efficiently at each step, and will typically result in very local updates of the grammar.

[8]Note: Our refinements of section 3.1 might also have been seen as intersections between a weighted FSA (rather than a weighted CFG) and a "local" automaton similar to "TwoDog", but their implementation was more direct.

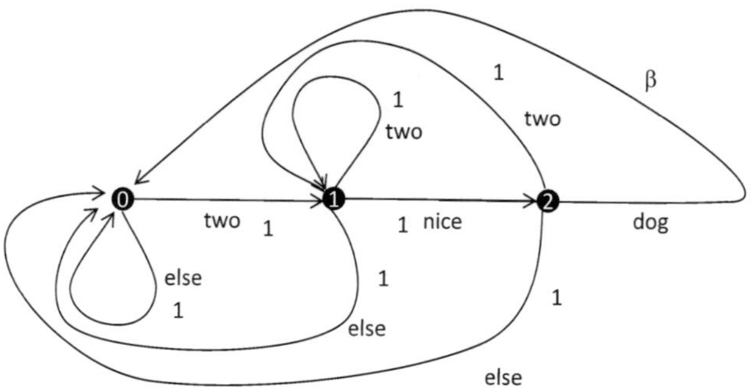

Figure 6: The "TwoNiceDog" automaton.

Higher-order n-grams can be registered in the grammar in a similar way. For instance, let's suppose that we have already incorporated in the grammar the knowledge of $w_2(dog|nice)$ and that we now wish to incorporate the knowledge of $w_3(dog|two\ nice)$, we can now use the following automaton ("TwoNiceDog" automaton), where $\beta = w_3(dog|two\ nice)/w_2(dog|nice)$:

For optimization, we thus find the maximum $x^{(i)}$ of each grammar $q^{(i)}$, check the ratio $p(x^{(i)})/q^{(i)}(x^{(i)})$, and stop if this ratio is close enough to 1. Else, we choose an n-gram in $x^{(i)}$ which is not yet registered and would significantly lower the proposal $q^{(i)}(x^{(i)})$ if added, build the automaton corresponding to this n-gram, and intersect this automaton with $q^{(i)}$.

Sampling is done in exactly the same way, the difference being that we now use dynamic programming to compute the *sum* of weights bottom-up in the grammars $q^{(i)}$, which is really a matter of using the sum-product semiring instead of the max-product semiring.

4 Conclusion

In this paper, we have argued for a unified viewpoint for heuristic optimization and rejection sampling, by using functional upper-bounds for both, and by using rejects as the basis for reducing the gap between the upper-bound and the objective. Bringing together Optimization and Sampling in this way permits to draw inspirations (A* Optimization, Rejection Sampling) from both domains to produce the joint algorithm OS*.

In particular, the optimization mode of OS*, which is directly inspired by rejection sampling, provides a generic exact optimization technique which appears to be more powerful than A* (as argued in section 2.6), and to have many potential applications to NLP distributions based on complex features, of which we detailed only two: high-order HMMs, and an agreement-based model for the combination of a weighted CFG with a language model. As these examples illustrate, often the same dynamic programming techniques can be used for optimization and sampling, the underlying representations being identical, the difference being only a change of semiring.

Both optimization and sampling are prominent questions in NLP generally, in the contexts of inference as well as of learning. In particular, we are currently working on applying these techniques to decoding and training tasks for phrase-based and also hierarchical statistical machine translation.

References

Christophe Andrieu, Nando de Freitas, Arnaud Doucet, and Michael I. Jordan. An introduction to MCMC for machine learning. *Machine Learning*, 50(1-2):5–43, 2003.

Y. Bar-Hillel, M. Perles, and E. Shamir. On formal properties of simple phrase structure grammars. *Zeitschrift für Phonetik, Sprachwissenschaft und Kommunicationsforschung*, 14: 143–172, 1961.

Simon Carter, Marc Dymetman, and Guillaume Bouchard. Exact Sampling and Decoding in High-Order Hidden Markov Models. In *Proceedings of the 2012 Joint Conference on Empirical Methods in Natural Language Processing and Computational Natural Language Learning*, pages 1125–1134, Jeju Island, Korea, July 2012. Association for Computational Linguistics. URL `http://www.aclweb.org/anthology/D12-1103`.

Yin-Wen Chang and Michael Collins. Exact decoding of phrase-based translation models through lagrangian relaxation. In *EMNLP*, pages 26–37, 2011.

M. Dymetman, G. Bouchard, and S. Carter. The OS* Algorithm: a Joint Approach to Exact Optimization and Sampling. *ArXiv e-prints*, July 2012.

W. R. Gilks and P. Wild. Adaptive rejection sampling for gibbs sampling. *Applied Statistics*, pages 337–348, 1992.

D. Görür and Y.W. Teh. Concave convex adaptive rejection sampling. Technical report, Gatsby Computational Neuroscience Unit, 2008.

P.E. Hart, N.J. Nilsson, and B. Raphael. A formal basis for the heuristic determination of minimum cost paths. *IEEE Transactions On Systems Science And Cybernetics*, 4(2): 100–107, 1968. URL `http://ieeexplore.ieee.org/lpdocs/epic03/wrapper.htm?arnumber=4082128`.

Zhiheng Huang, Yi Chang, Bo Long, Jean-Francois Crespo, Anlei Dong, Sathiya Keerthi, and Su-Lin Wu. Iterative viterbi a* algorithm for k-best sequential decoding. In *ACL (1)*, pages 611–619, 2012.

Nobuhiro Kaji, Yasuhiro Fujiwara, Naoki Yoshinaga, and Masaru Kitsuregawa. Efficient Staggered Decoding for Sequence Labeling. In *Meeting of the Association for Computational Linguistics*, pages 485–494, 2010.

Anthony C. Kam and Gary E. Kopec. Document image decoding by heuristic search. *IEEE Transactions on Pattern Analysis and Machine Intelligence*, 18:945–950, 1996.

S. Kirkpatrick, C. D. Gelatt, and M. P. Vecchi. Optimization by simulated annealing. *Science*, 220:671–680, 1983.

Philipp Koehn. Europarl: A parallel corpus for statistical machine translation. In *Proceedings of Machine Translation Summit*, pages 79–86, 2005.

Mark-Jan Nederhof and Giorgio Satta. Probabilistic parsing. In *New Developments in Formal Languages and Applications*, pages 229–258, 2008.

M.J. Nederhof and G. Satta. Probabilistic parsing as intersection. In *Proc. 8th International Workshop on Parsing Technologies*, 2003.

Slav Petrov. *Coarse-to-Fine Natural Language Processing*. PhD thesis, University of California at Berkeley, 2009.

K. Popat, D. Bloomberg, and D. Greene. Adding linguistic constraints to document image decoding. In *Proc. 4th International Workshop on Document Analysis Systems*. International Association of Pattern Recognition, December 2000.

Lawrence R. Rabiner. A tutorial on hidden markov models and selected applications in speech recognition. *Proceedings of the IEEE*, 77(2):257–286, February 1989.

Sebastian Riedel and James Clarke. Incremental integer linear programming for non-projective dependency parsing. In *Proceedings of the 2006 Conference on Empirical Methods in Natural Language Processing*, pages 129–137, Sydney, Australia, July 2006. Association for Computational Linguistics. URL `http://www.aclweb.org/anthology/W/W06/W06-1616`.

Christian P. Robert and George Casella. *Monte Carlo Statistical Methods (Springer Texts in Statistics)*. Springer-Verlag New York, Inc., Secaucus, NJ, USA, 2004. ISBN 0387212396.

Walter Rudin. *Real and Complex Analysis*. McGraw-Hill, 1987.

Alexander M. Rush and Michael Collins. Exact decoding of syntactic translation models through lagrangian relaxation. In *ACL*, pages 72–82, 2011.

Alexander M. Rush, David Sontag, Michael Collins, and Tommi Jaakkola. On dual decomposition and linear programming relaxations for natural language processing. In *Proceedings EMNLP*, 2010.

Steven L. Scott. Bayesian methods for hidden markov models: Recursive computing in the 21st century. *Journal of the American Statistical Association*, 97:337–351, 2002. URL `http://EconPapers.repec.org/RePEc:bes:jnlasa:v:97:y:2002:m:march:p:337-351`.

Andreas Stolcke. Srilm - an extensible language modeling toolkit. In *Proceedings of the International Conference of Spoken Language Processing (INTERSPEECH 2002)*, pages 257–286, 2002.

Roy W. Tromble and Jason Eisner. A fast finite-state relaxation method for enforcing global constraints on sequence decoding. In *Proceedings of the Human Language Technology Conference of the North American Association for Computational Linguistics (HLT-NAACL)*, pages 423–430, New York, June 2006. URL `http://cs.jhu.edu/~jason/papers/#tromble-eisner-2006`.

C. S. Wetherell. Probabilistic languages: A review and some open questions. *ACM Comput. Surv.*, 12(4):361–379, 1980. ISSN 0360-0300. doi: http://doi.acm.org/10.1145/356827.356829.

Iterative Chinese Bi-gram Term Extraction Using Machine-learning Classification Approach

Chia-Ming LEE[1], *Chien-Kang HUANG*[1], *Kuo-Ming TANG*[1]
(1) Department of Engineering Science and Ocean Engineering, National Taiwan University, Taipei, Taiwan (R.O.C.)
trueming@gmail.com, ckhuang@ntu.edu.tw, d965251013@ntu.edu.tw

ABSTRACT

This paper presents an iterative approach to extracting Chinese terms. Unlike the traditional approach to extracting Chinese terms, which requires the assistance of a dictionary, the proposed approach exploits the Support Vector Machine classifier which learns the extraction rules from the occurrences of a single popular term in the corpus. Additionally, we have designed a very effective feature set and a systematic approach for selecting the positive and negative samples as the source of training. An ancient Chinese corpus, Chinese Buddhist Texts, was taken as the experiment corpus. According to our experiment results, the proposed approach can achieve a very competitive result in comparison with the Chinese Knowledge and Information Processing (CKIP) system from Academia Sinica.

KEYWORDS : Chinese Term Extraction, Iterative Term Extraction, Support Vector Machine (SVM), Contextual Information, Single String Term Extraction.

Proceedings of the First International Workshop on Optimization Techniques for Human Language Technology, pages 95–108,
COLING 2012, Mumbai, December 2012.

1 Introduction

Chinese Term Extraction (CTE) is a fundamental issue in Chinese natural language processing studies. Existing research on term extraction evolved from two different types of corpora: pure-text corpora and labeled corpora (L.-F. Chien, 1997). In addition to the pure text, the labeled corpora contain an abundance of known information, such as terms, parts of speech, or even the syntactic tree structure. Grammar-based term extraction approaches are conventionally used with a labeled corpus (L.-F. Chien, 1997), and character-statistics-based term extraction approaches are usually used with pure-text corpora. However, both existing term extraction approaches need additional known information, prepared as supplements, which are independent from the corpus itself, and on principle, the more known information is prepared, the better the quality of the extracted terms. For instance, terms and part-of-speech labels within labeled corpora and dictionaries for verifying candidate terms found during the process of extracting terms from a pure-text corpus are usually additional prepared information.

Because all existing studies require more known information, this paper proposes the design of a process that extracts terms from a pure-text corpus without any additional information, especially known terms. In order to extract terms without a dictionary or other supplemental information, we introduce an iterative machine-learning term-extraction process. In this process, a Support Vector Machine (SVM) is exploited as the core of our learning mechanism. In order to extract terms starting from one specified term, the first step of our proposed approach is to generate the positive and negative examples with the one specified term and train an optimized SVM classification model with the proposed "term features" from an experimental corpus. Then, we can use the model to extract terms from the same corpus. In the iterative process, the previous results of the SVM term extraction are prepared as the training samples for the next SVM term extraction iteration. In our experiment, we specified one popular term as the initial learning sample and revealed the increasing rate of extracted terms of each iteration. The performance evaluation of the proposed approach was achieved by comparing the terms extracted using the iterative process with the terms verified by experts in chosen paragraphs from the experimental corpus.

In previous works, machine-learning algorithms have been used in many term-extraction studies. However, they have all extracted from labeled corpora with abundant known information (details are in the "Related Works" section). On the other hand, the concept of using an iterative process also has been proposed in other term-extraction research. For instance, the iterative model has been adopted by researchers studying the Sinica Corpus(Institute of Information Science and CKIP group in Academia Sinica, Since 1990). They used a segmentation tool to increase the term database, and then they further enhanced the segmentation tool with a larger term database. In our iterative approach, we have addressed a very extreme situation: starting from a single specified term.

In order to focus on the proposed idea of generating a learning sample, adding a contextual information extension, and developing an iterative extraction process, we executed the bi-gram CTE on a Middle Ages Chinese corpus, because bi-gram terms are the major part of Chinese texts (A. Chen, He, Xu, Gey, & Meggs, 1997) and also of the corpus used in our experiment[1].

[1] The book index of the corpus we used for our experiment [15] listed 404 uni-gram terms, 2678 bi-gram terms, 2227 tri-gram terms, 2404 quadri-gram terms, and 3334 other terms.

From the perspective of the machine-learning approach, terms with different lengths in a CTE might have some unique features that provide better classification results, and we leave studying these to our future work.

2 Related Works

Existing CTE research developed from studies using two types of corpora: labeled corpora and pure-text corpora. Labeled corpora are word-segmented corpora and usually contain abundant grammar information, such as parts of speech and even syntactic structures. The major purpose of a labeled-corpus CTE is to identify unknown words, also called out-of-vocabulary (OOV) terms, and to solve word-segmentation mistakes caused by natural language ambiguity problems in a corpus. Because labeled corpora contain grammar information, labeled-corpus CTE studies usually applied the grammar-based approaches. Other studies conducted serial unknown word identification on the Sinica Corpus (Sinica, Since 1990) using morphology rules (K.-J. Chen & Bai, 1998; K.-J. Chen & Ma, 2002; Ma & Chen, 2003).

The other type of corpora is pure-text corpora, which are growing with increased usage of text digitization and the World-Wide Web. The purpose of conducting a CTE on pure-text corpora is to recognize keywords, key phrases (L.-F. Chien, 1997; L. Chien, 1999), or domain-specific terms in a specific corpus. Because pure-text corpora are not accompanied by additional known information, character statistic-based approaches were usually used for CTEs of pure-text corpora. Therefore, many statistical patterns of Chinese terms have been proposed. For example, Chien's "Completed Lexicon Pattern" (L.-F. Chien, 1997) is a simple and effective design of Chinese terms in context, in which association and left and right context dependency were included.

2.1 Existing Machine-Learning Algorithms Used for Term Extraction

Many machine-learning algorithms are used in the study of CTE. The Hidden Markov Model (HMM) was used widely, because it is effective for modeling natural languages. Yu et al. (Yu, Zhang, Liu, Lv, & Shi, 2006) used different layers of HMMs to identify names of people, locations, and organizations in the ICTCLAS (Institute of Computing Technology Chinese Academy of Sciences, Since 2002) corpus. Cen et al. trained dual HMMs—a POS labeling model and a term boundary labeling model—to extract domain-specific terms (Cen, Han, & Ji, 2008). Xie et al. used a lexical chain of semantic relationships to extract key phrases from news-oriented Web pages (Xie, Wu, Hu, & Wang, 2008). However, all of the existing CTE research applied HMMs on labeled corpora, because labeled corpora have additional information, such as parts of speech or semantic relationships, which correspond to node-state patterns in the HMM.

Another popular machine learning algorithm used for CTE is the Support Vector Machine (SVM). Different from an HMM, the SVM is a multi-vector classification algorithm (Boser, Guyon, & Vapnik, 1992), and it is also a 2-phrase algorithm that employs a model-training phrase and a model-using (predicting) phrase. The major task of using the SVM is selecting a learning sample and a sample feature. Several researchers have used the SVM for CTE with the CoNLL-2000 Chunking Corpus (Sang & Buchholz, 2000): Goh used the SVM for recognizing person's names (Ling, Asahara, & Matsumoto, 2003). It used family names, contextual chunked marks and parts of speech as sample features. Li et al. extracted bi-gram and tri-gram terms using the SVM (Li, Huang, Gao, & Fan, 2005). The sample features they used were in-word probability of a character (IWP), analogy to new words, anti-word list, and frequency. The previously mentioned

CTE research studies still conducted extraction with a labeled corpus. However, this paper proposes a process to extract terms in a pure-text corpus using the SVM, and it also proposes a method of selecting a learning sample and a feature without additional known information.

3 Iterative Machine-Learning Term Extraction

Under the precondition of performing extraction without known information other than texts, the first problem in this machine-learning extraction process is how to generate sufficient number of good representational learning samples and sample features from a closed corpus. This section introduces a "negative sample selection" process, which fulfills the need to have a high capacity of differentiation in the known information. Also, a sufficient number of contextual lexicon parameters were added into the sample features in order to heighten the differentiation ability of the known information.

When considering the iterative process, we designed the process to increase the number of learning samples by filtering the extraction results during each iteration of the process. Therefore, this section will discuss three iterative issues: initial learning sample selection, iterative learning sample filtering, and the last convergence conditions of the entire iterative process.

3.1 Structure of the Iterative Machine-Learning Term-Extraction Process

There are six steps within the three phases of the iterative machine-learning term extraction process (see numbers 1 through 6 in the chart below). The first phase, also Step 1, is the initial selection of known information, the one known term. The second phase, the SVM machine-learning term extraction, includes Steps 2, 3, and 4. In Step 2, the SVM input dataset, in which data is in the form of positive/negative sample-features, is transformed and generated from the known information. The output of Step 3, SVM model training, is a sample classification model, which is used in step 4, SVM predicting, to extract terms from unknown strings in the corpus. Unknown strings, in the bi-gram extraction process, are all bi-gram strings in the corpus, and all unknown strings also need to be translated into a sample-features dataset for SVM predicting.

The iterative process stops when the increase of the term sizes between two subsequent SVM outputs is less than 2%, and it is checked in Step 5. For the next round of the iterative extraction process, Step 6 filters out initial known terms from the SVM output terms. The third phrase, evaluation, starts when the iterative process stops. The evaluation method compares the extracted terms from the iterative process with verified terms by experts and judges their precision, recall rate, and f-measure. The iterative processing chart is depicted in Figure 1.

3.2 Initial Known Information Selection

In Step 1, initial selection, the most frequent term in the corpus used in the experiment was selected as the initial known term. Although there was only one initial term, the available number of actual learning samples is the same as the word frequency of the initial term, because learning samples are contextually dependent. In this way, we were able to ensure the appropriate size of the initial learning samples.

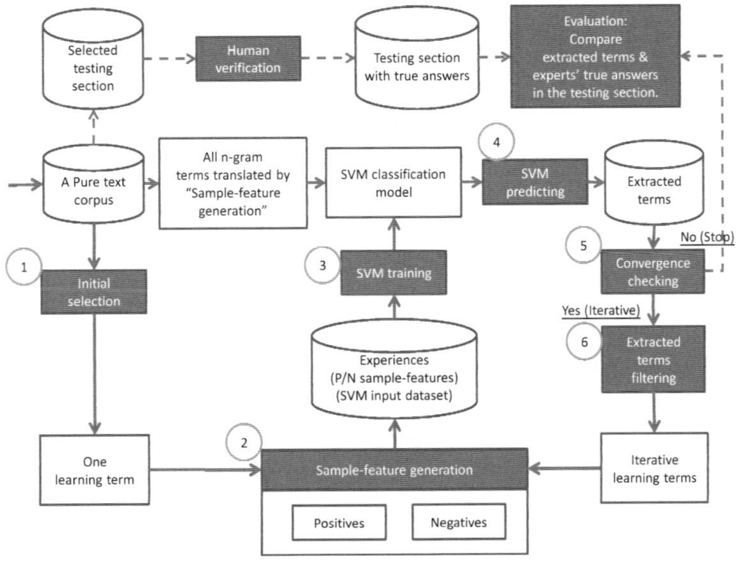

FIGURE 1 – The iterative machine-learning term-extraction process

3.3 Sample-feature Generation

Sample-feature Generation, step 2, generates learning samples from the initial known term(s) and feature parameters from each learning sample. There are three main components of sample-feature generation: (1) positive and negative learning sample generation, (2) lexicon features selection, and (3) contextual information extension.

3.3.1 Positive and Negative Sample Selection.

In this term extraction process, learning samples include positive samples and negative samples. Positive samples are the strings in which selected initial term(s) are located in a corpus. Negative samples are the new strings produced from shifting one character to the right or to the left in the context of the positive samples. In this way, every positive sample typically comes with two negative samples, and this can increase the number of learning samples, which is beneficial for the processing of the SVM classification algorithm. More importantly, shifting one character in context can break the lexicon pattern of the original sample, and this fulfills the need to have a high capacity of differentiation within the learning samples. Figure 2 shows a positive sample and its two negative sample selections.

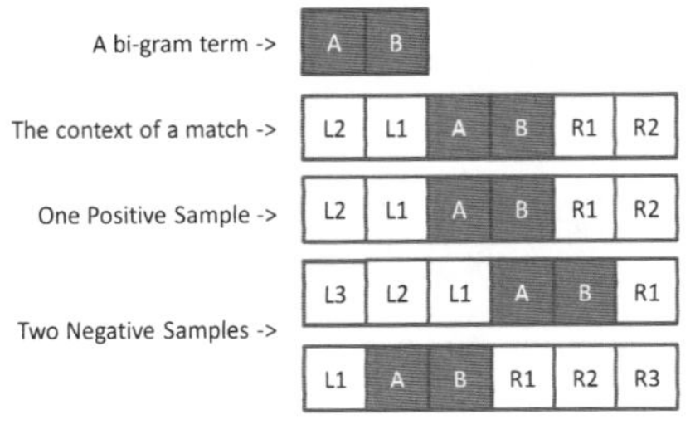

FIGURE 2 – Positive and negative sample selection

3.3.2 Features Selection

There are 10 types of features chosen for a learning sample in this extraction process, including frequency, the number of distinct characters to the left and right of the learning sample, the number of breaking symbols (non-Chinese characters and paragraph marks) to the left and right of the learning sample, association, and the usage of freedom to the left and right of the learning sample. Among these features, association and the usage of freedom (also called left and right context dependency) refer to the "estimation of complete lexical patterns" proposed by Chien (L.-F. Chien, 1997), as shown in Figure 3.

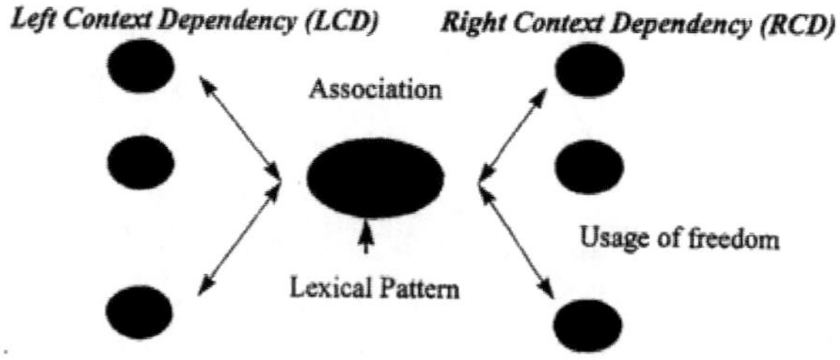

FIGURE 3 – The estimation of complete lexical patterns (L.-F. Chien, 1997)

Each of the lexical patterns is estimated using Equations 1, 2, and 3, as described below:

$$\text{Association (AEc)} = f(x) \,/\, (f(y) + f(z) - f(x)) \quad (1)$$

Where x is the lexical pattern to be estimated; $x = x_1, x_2, \ldots, x_n$, y and z are the two longest composed substrings of x with length n–1; $y = x_1, \ldots, x_{n-1}$, $z = x_2, \ldots, x_n$. Then, $f(x)$ is the frequency of x, $f(y)$ is the frequency of y and $f(z)$ is the frequecny of z.

$$\text{Left Context Dependency (LCD)} = f(\max\_x_L) \,/\, f(x) \quad (2)$$

$f(\max\_x_L)$ is the maximum frequency of the occurrence of distinct characters to the left of the lexical pattern x.

$$\text{Right Context Dependency (RCD)} = f(\max\_x_R) \,/\, f(x) \quad (3)$$

$f(\max\_x_R)$ is the maximum frequency of the occurrence of distinct characters to the right of the lexical pattern x.

The list of the 10 types of features are shown in Table 1.

1.	Frequency
2.	The number of distinct character to the left
3.	The maximum occurrence frequency of distinct character to the left
4.	The number of breaking symbols to the left
5.	The number of distinct character to the right
6.	The maximum occurrence frequency of distinct character to the right
7.	The number of breaking symbols to the right
8.	Association: AEc
9.	Left-context dependency (LCD)
10.	Right-context dependency (RCD)

TABLE 1 – Feature list

3.3.3 Contextual Feature Extension

The concept of contextual information has often been used in information extraction research as well as in existing CTE research for entity identification (Ji, Sum, Lu, Li, & Chen, 2007; Ling et al., 2003). In order to enhance the effect of contextual information on the classification results, in our study, the initial learning samples (also called original samples) were designed to extend into longer learning samples. Then, the features of every bi-gram within the new samples, as shown in Table 1, are collected as the contextual information of the original samples. According to the result of the experiments, not included in this paper, the best length of the longer learning samples was two characters on both the left and right sides. For instance, an original bi-gram learning sample will extend to become a 6-gram learning sample, and the feature parameter will become five times larger than before, because there will be 5 bi-grams within the new sample. Table 2 shows the differences of sample lengths and feature parameters before and after the contextual extension.

Before	After
Original n-gram learning sample: A B	Extended learning sample: L2 L1 A B R1 R2
Contextual bi-gram set: 0	Contextual bi-gram set: 4 L2 L1 L1 A B R1 R1 R2
Number of original features: 10 10 features (see Table 1) for A B.	Number of original features: 10 10 features (see Table 1) for A B. extend Number of contextual info. features: 40 10 features (see Table 1) for each extended bi-gram, L2 L1 L1 A B R1 R1 R2

TABLE 2 – Contextual feature extension

In addition to the features in Table 2, to increase the number of features of the contextual information, we also added into the feature set all uni-gram frequencies within an extended learning sample. Therefore, an extended bi-gram learning sample, a 6-gram string, will actually have a total of 56 features, including six uni-gram frequencies and 50 features coming from five bi-gram feature sets.

3.4 SVM Machine-Learning Term Extraction

The Support Vector Machine (SVM) algorithm constructs a hyper-plane in a high-dimensional space for classification or other tasks. A good separation is achieved by the hyper-plane farthest from the nearest training data point of any class.

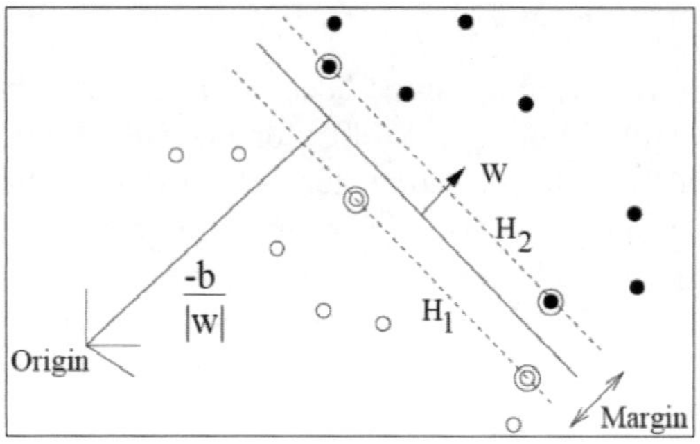

FIGURE 4 – Support Vector Machine (SVM)

In Figure 4, W is the good separation (the classification hyper-plane) of the two classes—white spots and black spots—and H1 and H2 are support hyper-planes.

$\mathbf{W}^T\mathbf{X}+b=0$, H1: $\mathbf{W}^T\mathbf{X}+b=1$, H2: $\mathbf{W}^T\mathbf{X}+b=-1$

To maximize the distance between H1 and H2 (2 / ||w||):

$$L(w,b,\alpha)=\frac{1}{2}\|w\|^2-\sum_{i=1}^{N}\alpha_i\left[y_i\left(w^T x_i+b\right)-1\right]$$

In our study, libsvm tools (Chang & Lin, 2011) were used to execute the SVM algorithm during the term-extraction process. The SVM algorithm includes two phases: model training and unknown-term predicting. In the model-training phase, the input data is the sample-feature dataset of learning samples generated from the sample feature generation step, and the output data is a classification model file. Meanwhile, all strings (not distinct) with the same length as the learning samples in the corpus are considered unknown samples. Unknown samples will convert to the sample-feature dataset in the exactly same way learning samples generation converts to its dataset. In the unknown-term-predicting phase, the input data is the sample-feature dataset of unknown samples and the classification model file output from the earlier phase, and the output data are unknown strings that are predicted as terms. The predicted output data are the term extraction results.

3.5 Iterative Convergence Condition

The stop condition of the iterative extraction process occurs when the increase between the term sizes from two subsequent extraction results is less than 2%.

3.6 Iterative Learning Sample Selection

Step 6, filtering, in Figure 1, filters the extracted terms, which will become learning samples for the next extraction round. The libsvm tools provide the function of probability estimation, predicting the probability of each unknown sample being classified into a certain category. In this step, the rate of probability is then adjusted to filter out the learning samples for the next round. According to the default setting in libsvm, an unknown sample is considered a term when its predicted probability rate is greater than or equal to 50%. Also, in this iterative extraction process, the learning samples for the next round are chosen when the predicted probability rate is greater than or equal to 90%.

3.7 Evaluation of the Term Extraction Results

In this paper, precision, recall, and f-measure were used to evaluate the effectiveness of the term extraction results. The correct answers were pre-decided by experts for a chosen paragraph in the corpus and then compared with the extraction results. The experts did not examine the extracted results directly. The evaluation results are shown in the next section.

4 The Experiment

As part of a Chinese text archive from the Middle Ages provided by the Chinese Buddhist Electronic Text Association (CBETA), the collection of Saddharma Puṇḍarīka (Lotus of the true Dharma) was used as the experimental corpus, which consists of 16 sutras labeled from T0262 to T0277 in the Taisho Revised Tripitaka. This corpus contains 514,722 Chinese characters, among which are 3,041 distinct uni-grams, 82,688 distinct bi-grams, and 202,187 distinct tri-grams. Generally, ancient Chinese corpora are rarely used in term extraction research due to the difficulty of collecting known information. However, for our study, the design of the initial known information selection and the contextual sample-features generation in the iterative learning process produced good extraction results regarding the ancient Chinese corpus.

Another reason for using Buddhist texts is that the Middle Age Chinese literature, of which the Buddhist canon is representative, is mainly composed by bi-gram terms, the same as is current Chinese literature (梁曉虹, 2005). So, theoretically this iterative term extraction process can be directly applied to other forms of current Chinese texts as well. The experiment in this section focuses on bi-gram term extraction from the collection of Saddharma Puṇḍarīka (CBETA) to list the iterative experiment results and further compares them with the results of other term extraction algorithms.

In the corpus, Sàtánfēntuólìjīng, a sutra (T0265) from the collection of Saddharma Puṇḍarīka, was chosen to be the evaluation text. In Sàtánfēntuólìjīng, there are 1,430 non-distinct bi-grams which have been prepared with experts' judgments of true bi-gram terms. The ratio size of the evaluation text is 0.32% of the entire corpus, which consists of 442,513 non-distinct bi-grams.

4.1 Iterative Term Extraction

This section shows the experimental results of the iterative extraction process. The size of the experimental corpus is 2,058,888 bytes. There are a total of 514722 symbols encoded by UTF-32, and 442513 non-distinct Chinese bi-grams in the corpus. The initial selected bi-gram term is 一切 and the number of initial learning samples are 2387, with the term frequency of 一切 in the corpus.

Table 3 shows the results of numbers of initial learning samples and SVM extraction terms, and increasing ratios of total and unique extraction terms in 8 rounds.

In Table 3, values in the "Extraction ratio" row are determined by the following equation:

$$\frac{\text{number of "SVM extraction terms"}}{442513\left(\text{the number of total bi-grams in the corpus used for our experiment}\right)}$$

Iterative Rounds	1	2	3	4	5	6	7	8
Initial learning samples	2387	18259	55360	120826	148781	160849	166583	169777
SVM extraction terms	18259	55360	120826	148781	160849	166583	169777	171570
Extraction ratio	4.126%	12.51%	27.30%	33.62%	36.34%	37.64%	38.36%	38.77%
Subsequent increasing ratio		+8.39%	+14.79%	+6.32%	+2.72%	+1.30% (<2.00%)	+0.72% (<2.00%)	+0.41% (<2.00%)
Unique extraction terms	15	1044	8148	12287	14679	16422	17520	18174
Unique terms increasing times		*69.60	*7.80	*1.50	*1.19	*1.12	*1.06	*1.04

TABLE 3 – The extraction convergence table

The "Subsequent increasing ratio" row shows increasing ratios of the "Extraction ratio" row. The "Unique extraction terms" row indicates the distinct number of "SVM extraction terms," and the "Unique terms increasing times" row shows the number of times the number of extracted distinct terms increased when compared to the previous round.

Based on the iterative experiment results, the sixth round should be the final extraction result in this experiment, because the saturation condition is set when the increase in the number of terms from one SVM to the next is less than 2%. Meanwhile, the states of the increase in number of the SVM extraction terms, the total bi-gram terms, and the Unique extraction terms are different. The increase of unique terms is about to saturate in the third round, which is two or three rounds before the saturation of the increase of total extraction terms.

4.2 Evaluation

In the corpus, Sàtánfēntuólìjīng (Tripitaka sutra number T0265) was chosen to be the texting data. There are 1,430 non-distinct Chinese bi-grams in Sàtánfēntuólìjīng, and the ratio size of the texting data is 0.32% of the entire corpus. In the testing data, the number of positive samples (expert verified bi-gram terms) is 332, and the number of negative samples (expert verified non-bi-gram terms) is 1098. The evaluation indices are listed below.

$$Precision = \frac{True\ Positive}{True\ Positive + False\ Positive}$$

$$Recall = \frac{True\ Positive}{True\ Positive + False\ Negative}$$

$$F\text{-}measure = \frac{2 \cdot Precision \cdot Recall}{Precision + Recall}$$

Iterative Rounds	True Positive	False Positive	False Negative	True Negative
1	26	3	306	1095
2	85	24	247	1074
3	201	128	131	970
4	235	188	97	910
5	251	219	81	879
6	255	228	77	870
7	256	234	76	864
8	257	238	75	860

TABLE 4 – Table of the classifier prediction compared to the experts' judgments

Iterative Rounds	Accuracy	Precision	Recall	F-measure
1	78.4%	89.7%	7.8%	14.35%
2	81.0%	78.0%	25.6%	38.54%
3	81.9%	61.1%	60.5%	60.79%
4	80.1%	55.6%	70.8%	62.28%
5	79.0%	53.4%	75.6%	62.58%
6	78.7%	52.8%	76.8%	62.57%
7	78.3%	52.2%	77.1%	62.25%
8	78.1%	51.9%	77.4%	62.13%

TABLE 5 – The evaluation calculation

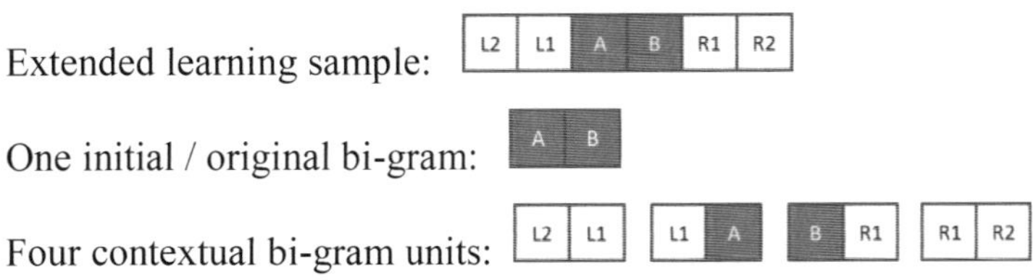

FIGURE 5 – The contextual bi-gram set

No.	Feature Explanation	F-source
1	RCD of A B	0.4420
2	LCD of A B	0.3304
3	LCD of B R1	0.3281
4	RCD of L1 A	0.3144
5	The number of distinct character to the left of A B	0.2284
6	The number of distinct character to the right of A B	0.2199
7	AEc of A B	0.2108
8	The number of distinct character to the left of B R1	0.1598
9	RCD of B R1	0.1513
10	The number of breaking symbols to the left of A B	0.1480
11	LCD of L1 A	0.1390
12	The number of distinct character to the right of L1 A	0.1338
13	The number of distinct character to the right of B R1	0.1295
14	Frequency of A B	0.1256
15	The number of distinct character to the left of L1 A	0.1123

TABLE 6 – Top 15 features sorted by f-score

4.3 Features Selection Analysis

This section analyzes the importance of features used in the SVM extraction process. A total of 56 features were calculated and sorted by the f-score algorithm proposed by Chen and Lin's SVM feature-selected research (Y.-W. Chen & Lin, 2006).

Figure 5 shows that one extended learning sample is represented by 5 bi-grams, including one original bi-gram and 4 contextual bi-grams. And Table 6, the top 15 features of training dataset, shows that the learning sample and contextual features extension has a great influence on the SVM classification extraction.

5 Comparison

This section discusses the comparison of the bi-gram term extraction results from three different term extraction algorithms with the verification answers by experts using the same corpus. The first set of results come from the iterative machine learning extraction process proposed by this paper. The second set is the control group using the same process with two controlled conditions: (1) using 2,678 known terms from the book index of the corpus (大藏經學術用語研究會, 198-?) as the initial known terms and (2) using no iterative extraction and executing the SVM extraction process only once. With this control group, we can compare the extraction differences between using known terms outside of the corpus and known terms trained iteratively inside of the corpus. The third extraction algorithm used for comparison is the Sinica CKIP system (Chinese Knowledge Information Processing Group), which represents the term segmentation and extraction algorithms based on a "term database."

In Table 7, the "MLTE iterative" row using the sixth round extraction results from the previous experiment, and the "MLTE_dic" row is the extraction result of the dictionary control group. The comparison table shows that the SVM algorithm with dictionary-known terms more effectively extracted terms, but the iterative SVM algorithm extraction had the highest recall rate, and both extraction results from the SVM algorithm had a higher F-measure values than the CKIP recognition results on bi-gram.

	Precision	Recall	F-measure
MLTE_dic	65.8%(202/307)	60.8%(202/332)	63.20 %
MLTE_iterative	52.8%(255/483)	76.8%(255/332)	62.58 %
CKIP	62.5%(203/325)	61.1%(203/332)	61.80 %

TABLE 7 – Comparison of 3 extraction results

6 Discussions

For this study, we proposed an iterative machine-learning term-extraction process that does not use known information other than the pure-text corpus itself. In this process, the effective selection of learning samples and sample features were designed specifically for two classes of SVM machine-learning algorithms. Based on the experimental results of this iterative extraction process, there are some issues and problems deserving further discussions:

1. The design of the process to extract n-gram terms of any given length. The current iterative process in this paper can only extract fixed-length n-gram terms. In order to extract terms of

any length and integrate the extraction results of terms of varied lengths, it is more ideal to directly design a method to extract samples and sample feature parameters for terms of any given length and to establish the extraction model.

2. The testing and discussion of the applicability of this iterative extraction process with different types of corpora, such as current Chinese texts or Web messages.
3. The discussion of the initial learning sample selection, which is a changeable parameter in the initial learning sample in this extraction process. Besides the most frequent terms in the corpus, if we use other high frequency terms or if we take into account other factors, such as parts of speech the process might provide different extraction results and issues for further discussion.

Acknowledgments

The authors would like to thank the National Science Council of the Republic of China, Taiwan, for financially supporting this research under Contract No. NSC 99-2410-H-002-203-MY2.

References

Boser, B. E., Guyon, I. M., & Vapnik, V. N. (1992). *A training algorithm for optimal margin classifiers*. Paper presented at the Proceedings of the fifth annual workshop on Computational learning theory, Pittsburgh, Pennsylvania, United States.

Cen, Y., Han, Z., & Ji, P. (2008). *Chinese Term Recognition and Extraction Based on Hidden Markov Model*. Paper presented at the Computational Intelligence and Industrial Application, 2008. PACIIA '08. Pacific-Asia Workshop on.

Chang, C.-C., & Lin, C.-J. (2011). LIBSVM: A library for support vector machines. *ACM Trans. Intell. Syst. Technol., 2*(3), 1-27. doi: 10.1145/1961189.1961199

Chen, A., He, J., Xu, L., Gey, F. C., & Meggs, J. (1997). *Chinese text retrieval without using a dictionary*. Paper presented at the Proceedings of the 20th annual international ACM SIGIR conference on Research and development in information retrieval, Philadelphia, Pennsylvania, United States.

Chen, K.-J., & Bai, M.-H. (1998). *Unknown Word Detection for Chinese by a Corpus-based Learning Method*. Paper presented at the Computational Linguistics and Chinese Language Processing.

Chen, K.-J., & Ma, W.-Y. (2002). *Unknown word extraction for Chinese documents*. Paper presented at the Proceedings of the 19th international conference on Computational linguistics - Volume 1, Taipei, Taiwan.

Chen, Y.-W., & Lin, C.-J. (2006). Combining SVMs with Various Feature Selection Strategies. *Feature Extraction - Studies in Fuzziness and Soft Computing, 207*, 315-324.

Chien, L.-F. (1997). *PAT-tree-based keyword extraction for Chinese information retrieval*. Paper presented at the Proceedings of the 20th annual international ACM SIGIR conference on Research and development in information retrieval, Philadelphia, Pennsylvania, United States.

Chien, L. (1999). PAT-tree-based adaptive keyphrase extraction for intelligent Chinese information retrieval. *Information Processing and Management, 35*(4), 501.

Chinese Knowledge Information Processing Group. CKIP Chinese Word Segmentation System, from http://ckipsvr.iis.sinica.edu.tw/

Institute of Computing Technology Chinese Academy of Sciences. (Since 2002). Institute of Computing Technology Chinese Lexical Analysis System (ICTCLAS). *ICTCLAS 2010*, from http://ictclas.org/

Institute of Information Science and CKIP group in Academia Sinica. (Since 1990). Academia Sinica Balanced Corpus of Modern Chinese. *Sinica Corpus 4.0*, from http://db1x.sinica.edu.tw/kiwi/mkiwi/

Ji, L., Sum, M., Lu, Q., Li, W., & Chen, Y. (2007). *Chinese Terminology Extraction Using Window-Based Contextual Information*. Paper presented at the CICLing 2007.

Li, H., Huang, C.-N., Gao, J., & Fan, X. (2005). The Use of SVM for Chinese New Word Identification

Natural Language Processing – IJCNLP 2004. In K.-Y. Su, J. i. Tsujii, J.-H. Lee & O. Kwong (Eds.), (Vol. 3248, pp. 723-732): Springer Berlin / Heidelberg.

Ling, G. C., Asahara, M., & Matsumoto, Y. (2003). *Chinese unknown word identification using character-based tagging and chunking*. Paper presented at the Proceedings of the 41st Annual Meeting on Association for Computational Linguistics - Volume 2, Sapporo, Japan.

Ma, W.-Y., & Chen, K.-J. (2003). *A bottom-up merging algorithm for Chinese unknown word extraction*. Paper presented at the Proceedings of the second SIGHAN workshop on Chinese language processing - Volume 17, Sapporo, Japan.

Sang, E. F. T. K., & Buchholz, S. (2000). *Introduction to the CoNLL-2000 shared task: chunking*. Paper presented at the Proceedings of the 2nd workshop on Learning language in logic and the 4th conference on Computational natural language learning - Volume 7, Lisbon, Portugal.

Sinica, I. o. I. S. a. C. g. i. A. (Since 1990). Academia Sinica Balanced Corpus of Modern Chinese. *Sinica Corpus 4.0*, from http://db1x.sinica.edu.tw/kiwi/mkiwi/

Xie, F., Wu, X., Hu, X.-G., & Wang, F.-Y. (2008). *Keyphrase Extraction from Chinese News Web Pages Based on Semantic Relations*. Paper presented at the Proceedings of the IEEE ISI 2008 PAISI, PACCF, and SOCO international workshops on Intelligence and Security Informatics, Taipei, Taiwan.

Yu, H.-k., Zhang, H.-p., Liu, Q., Lv, X.-q., & Shi, S.-c. (2006). Chinese named entity identification using cascaded hidden Markov model. *Journal on Communications, 27-2*, 8.

大藏經學術用語研究會. (198-?). *大藏經索引*. 台北: 新文豐.

梁曉虹, 徐., 陳五雲. (2005). *佛經音義與漢語詞彙研究*. 北京: 北京商務印書館.

Parameter estimation under uncertainty with Simulated Annealing applied to an ant colony based probabilistic WSD algorithm

Andon TCHECHMEDJIEV[1] *Didier SCHWAB*[1] *Jérôme GOULIAN*[1]
Gilles SÉRASSET[1]
(1) Univ. Grenoble-Alpes, LIG-GETALP, France
{andon.tchechmedjiev, didier.schwab, jerome.goulian, gilles.serasset}@imag.fr

ABSTRACT
In this article we propose a method based on simulated annealing for the parameter estimation of probabilistic algorithms, where the solution provided by the algorithm can vary from execution to execution. Such algorithms are often very interesting to solve complex combinatorial problems, yet they involve many parameters that can be difficult to estimate manually due to their randomized output. We applied and evaluated a method for the parameter estimation of such algorithms and applied it for an Ant Colony Algorithm for WSD. For the evaluation, we used the Semeval 2007 Task 7 corpus. We split the corpus and took in turn one text as a training corpus and the four remaining texts as a test corpus. We tuned the parameters with an increasing number of sentences from the training text in order to estimate the quantity of data necessary to obtain an efficient and general set of parameters. We found that the results greatly depend on the nature of the text, even a very small amount of training sentences can lead to good results if the text has the right properties.

RÉSUMÉ (French)
Estimation de paramètres à base de Recuit Simulé sous incertitude appliquée à un algorithmes à colonies de fourmis probabiliste.
Nous proposons une méthode basée sur un Recuit Simulé pour l'estimation de paramètres pour des algorithmes probabilistes où les solutions générées varient. Ces algorithmes sont souvent très intéressant pour la résolution de problèmes combinatoires complexes, mais ils requièrent de nombreux paramètres pouvant être difficiles à estimer manuellement à cause de la nature aléatoire des solutions. Nous avons appliquésPlus spécifiquement, nous appliquons et évaluons cette méthode à pour estimer les paramètres de tels algorimes et l'appliquons à un Algorithme à Colonies de Fourmis pour la désambiguïsation lexicale. Pour l'évaluation, nous avons utilisé le corpus de Semeval 2007 Tâche 7. Nous avons repectivement séparé un texte comme corpus d'entraînement et les quatre autres comme corpus de test. Nous estimons les paramètres pour un nombre croissant de phrases pour déterminer combien de données sont nécessaires pour obtenir un ensemble de valeurs de paramètres générales et efficaces. Nous concluons que la qualité des résultats dépends de la nature des textes. Même des petites quantités de de phrases peuvent suffir à obtenir de bons résultats, du moment que le texte à les bonnes propriètés.

KEYWORDS: Word Sense Disambiguation, Parameter Estimation, Simulated Annealing, Uncertainty, Stochastic Algorithms.

KEYWORDS IN FR: Désabiguïsation Lexicale, Estimation de Paramètres, Recuit Simulé, Incertitude, Algorithmes Stocastiques.

Proceedings of the First International Workshop on Optimization Techniques for Human Language Technology, pages 109–124,
COLING 2012, Mumbai, December 2012.

1 Introduction

Word Sense Disambiguation (WSD) is a very difficult yet central task in Natural Language Processing (NLP), that pertains to the labelling of the words of a text with the senses that most closely match the context. Numerous approaches exist to tackle WSD, yet many of these methods have in common a sizeable complexity, reflected by a number of parameters that need to be tuned in order to obtain the best performance. Depending on the number of parameters, it can be very difficult for a human to directly estimate the optimal parameters. Even then, it remains a question of guesswork with no guarantee of success.

This issue is all the more salient with algorithms and models that typically involve many parameters upon which the results greatly depend. Such algorithms for WSD include Neural Networks (Veronis and Ide, 1990), Simulated Annealing (SA) (Cowie et al., 1992), Genetic Algorithms (GA) (Gelbukh et al., 2003) and Ant Colony Algorithms (ACA) (Schwab and Guillaume, 2011), and many other machine learning methods.

In such approaches, the values of the parameters are paramount. They are what make the algorithms work for specific applications such as WSD. Yet, the authors of the aforementioned articles give little insight as to how the parameters are determined. They only provide the "best" values. Although a *trial and error* approach is a good start when devising an algorithm or tailoring it to a new application, it makes the adaptation and the scalability of such systems an issue. Naturally, for well known and understood algorithms such as Simulated Annealing, there are some theoretical criteria to select the parameters. However, the process remains to be repeated for every new setting and can be tedious to perform.

Furthermore, even with few parameters, evaluating all possible parameter configurations is a prohibitively long process. For example, in the case of a stochastic algorithm with 10 parameters that have 20 possible values each, assuming the algorithm needs to be run 100 times (due to its stochastic nature) and that one execution takes on average 30 seconds, the time necessary to evaluate all parameter combinations is $20^{12} \cdot 100 \times 30 = 3 \times 10^{15} s$ which is almost 1 billion years! Thus, the advantages of considering automated or adaptive heuristic approaches to the estimation of parameters are clear.

In the case of a deterministic algorithm, many combinatorial optimisation methods can be used with little effort. However, due to the complexity of WSD, many approaches are statistical or probabilistic in nature and the use classical combinatorial optimization heuristics becomes impossible. Therefore, we adapt the classical simulated annealing algorithm to work for an uncertain objective function based on the ideas of (Painton and Diwekar, 1995), by using standard non-parametric statistical significance tests.

First, we present the tools and the metrics for the evaluation of WSD, followed by the description of the Ant Colony Algorithm considered in this article. Then, we briefly survey other approaches for parameter estimation under uncertainty and express the problem formally. Subsequently, we present the general formulation or simulated annealing and different aspects pertaining to it and then present its adaptation to uncertain objective function. We then present and analyse our experimental protocol and the results of the experiments. Finally, we conclude on the results and draw some perspectives for future research.

2 Evaluation of WSD Systems

The use of Precision and Recall constitutes the standard evaluation metrics for WSD systems.

Precision represents the number of correctly disambiguated words among all the attempted words, while Recall represents the number of correctly disambiguated words among all the ambiguous words in the document. It is customary to compute the F1 score between Precision and Recall as $\frac{2 \cdot P \cdot R}{P+R}$, in order to have a single evaluation metric that equally captures the information conveyed by both Precision and Recall.

In this work in particular we use the Semeval 2007 Task 7 all words coarse grained corpus for the evaluation of the quality of the disambiguation. The all-words task provides a corpus of texts, where in each text all ambiguous words (T) need to be disambiguated by tagging them with Wordnet 2.1 sense keys. An algorithm must correctly tag as many ambiguous words as possible (TP) depending on the context. A sense is considered correct if the sense key assigned to it matches the sense provided in the gold standard or any of its subsumed senses (hence coarse-grained). If we write the number of incorrectly assigned senses as (TN), then, for this particular task, precision can be expressed as $P = \frac{TP}{TP+TN}$ and recall as $R = \frac{TP}{T}$

The choice of the all words task in particular is based on the functioning of the algorithm that is more adapted to a globally coherent text, rather than independent sentences or words. As such, the metrics available for the evaluation are Precision, Recall and F-measure, which leads to some important restrictions on the methods or criteria available for parameter estimation as will be detailed in the subsequent sections.

3 Context: an ant colony algorithm for WSD

The ant colony algorithm presented by (Schwab and Guillaume, 2011) and (Schwab et al., 2012) that our work focuses on, offers some interesting properties regarding the quality of the solutions, which are on par with state-of-the-art knowledge rich WSD systems, combined with a fast execution time compared to the latter systems. Furthermore, it is also well suited to working on full texts at a time with a full annotation coverage.

Moreover, its stochastic nature leads to the generation of solutions with variable precision scores, which is usually not a very sought after property in algorithms. However, this variability enables the use of voting strategies that lead to results approaching supervised WSD systems and overcome the elusive (for unsupervised and knowledge-based systems) First Sense Baseline. Due to the quick execution time (in the 60s to 65s range), voting strategies can directly be applied while still leading to cumulative execution times for several executions that are lower to that of other systems.

However, those qualities are also a major disadvantage when it comes to selecting and tuning the parameters of the algorithm. Not only are there relatively many, but they can only be determined manually to some extent through painstaking trial and error modifications, with no guarantees of optimality. Notwithstanding with the fact that the stochastic nature of the algorithm makes it rather impractical to determine whether the improvement resulting from a given parameter change is simply due to random variations of the solution distribution or really to significant variations.

3.1 Parameter model

Let us now review the various parameters of the system, their typical value ranges and meaningful increments. The parameters are summarized in Table 2. There are seven parameters in total, five of which are discrete and represented by integers and two continuous parameters represented as positive real numbers between zero and one.

Given the number of parameters, even with some knowledge about how the algorithm works, one can at best chose sensible parameter value ranges in order to limit the combinatorial explosion.

Initially, before the estimation method proposed in this paper, we determined the values of some parameters by making iterative and independent changes. Of course such an approach is limited due to the fact that it is a heuristic based on the assumption that the parameters of the system are independent. For ACA it is in fact the opposite, as it is with other methods.

The values obtained through this process were $\omega = 10$, $E_a = 1$, $E_{max} = 8$, $E_0 = 10$, $\delta_v = 0.9$, $\delta = 0.9$, $L_V = 90$ and yielded results around 75% on the Semeval 2007 Task 7 corpus (Schwab and Guillaume, 2011).

Furthermore, given the number of parameters and their value ranges, an exhaustive enumeration is intractable. If we calculate the number of combinations (assuming 0.01 steps for continuous variables), we obtain $60 \times 60 \times 100 \times 55 \times 25 \times 35 \times 100 = 17325 \cdot 10^8$ combinations. Knowing that due to the stochastic nature we may need to make at least 50 or 100 executions, we get to $17325 \cdot 10^9$ combinations.

Notation	Description	Value	Exploration granularity
E_a	Energy taken by an ant when it arrives on a node	1–60	1
E_{max}	Maximum quantity of energy an ant can carry	1–60	1
δ_ϕ	Evaporation rate of the pheromone between two cycles	0.0–1.0	0.01
E_0	Initial quantity of energy on each node	5–60	1
ω	Ant life-span	5–30 (cycles)	1
L_V	Odour vector length	20–200	5
δ_V	Ratio of odour vector components (words) deposited by an ant when it arrives on a node	0.0–1.0	0.01

Table 2: Parameters of the Ant Colony Algorithm and their typical value-ranges

Assuming leaps in computational power or heavy parallelism that would make the algorithm take only one second to run, the search for the optimal parameters would still take 549372 years.

For this reason, we are interested in finding and automated way of estimating the *optimal* parameters. Of course, when dealing with linguistic data, there is no such thing as *optimal*. By *optimal*, we merely mean a set of parameters that yield results with F-scores as high as can be achieved.

4 Related work

In the context of this article, when considering WSD algorithm evaluated as described in Section 2, the output of the evaluation of the algorithm output is simply a F-score percentage. In order to apply classical estimation theory approaches (Kay, 1993), we would need to either find a model of the posterior PDF, or to empirically estimate it. However, given the size of the search space and the cost of running the algorithm, this would be very much equivalent to making an exhaustive search. Furthermore, the relationship between the values of the parameters and the resulting scores are non-linear. However, there are some models that attempt to provide a probability distribution for precision, recall, and F-measure for information retrieval that could potentially be applied to WSD (Goutte and Gaussier, 2005).

In fact, it is much simpler to treat the estimation as a combinatorial optimisation problem, by attempting to simply maximize the f-score value. In this context, given that we want the ability to handle many parameters that can take many discrete values, we need to consider heuristics for an efficient estimation of complex non-linear multivariate functions.

A popular choices for parameter estimation are Genetic Algorithms (GA) or Simulated annealing (SA) among others. For instance, GAs have been widely applied, either in a general parameter estimation context, such as in (Sharman and McClurkin, 1989), (Yao and Sethares, 1994) or (Paterakis et al., 1998); or for specific application domains such as robotics (Bolhasani, 2004), applied statistics (Pan et al., 1995), meteorology (Lee et al., 2006), chemistry (Katare et al., 2004) and many others.

For WSD, (Daelemans et al., 2003) and (Decadt et al., 2004) have also proposed to use GAs for joint parameter estimation and feature selection. Although joint optimisation is very interesting, it is application and task specific, and would be difficult to implement in a probabilistic setting.

All the techniques mentioned above are meant to optimise a deterministic objective function. When the objective function itself is uncertain or noisy, instead of a single value, one has a set of observation samples with different values that have to be dealt with. The main issues are the question of how to know what value to consider for the maximisation and how to take the variability into account to avoid effects due to random chance.

One model of *stochastic* simulated annealing has been proposed in (Painton and Diwekar, 1995) and then further extended in (Kim and Diwekar, 2002), where the evaluation function is sampled several times, and the expected value is incorporated into a modified objective function, with the variance acting a penalty term.

5 Problem formalization

Before describing the parameter estimation algorithm, it is important to formulate in a more formal and generic way the parameter model of any WSD algorithm with a randomized output.

Let $\vec{\theta} = [\theta_1, \theta_2, \ldots, \theta_i, \ldots \theta_n] \in \Theta$, be the parameter model of a WSD algorithm, where $\Theta = \Theta_1 \times \Theta_2 \times \ldots \times \Theta_i \times \ldots \times \Theta_n$ and each Θ_i is a finite discrete set of integers or a bounded real range.

For example, in the case of the parameter model of the ant colony algorithm, the general form of θ would be $\theta = \{\omega, E_a, E_{max}, E_0, \delta_v, \delta, L_V\}$. The initial set of parameters would be an instance written as $\theta_I = \{10, 1, 8, 10, 0.9, 0.9, 90\}$.

We can represent a deterministic WSD system with a function WSD_C, that for a given corpus C and a parameter vector $\vec{\theta}$[1] returns a $F-score$ value between 0 and 1:

$$WSD_C : \Theta \rightarrow 0 \leq x \in \mathbb{R} \leq 1 \tag{1}$$

$$\theta \mapsto F_{score} \tag{2}$$

Thus, the problem of finding the best θ, θ^* can be formalized as follows:

$$\theta^* = \arg\max_{\theta \in \Theta} WSD_C(\theta) \tag{3}$$

In other words, if we define a sequence θ_n that enumerates possible parameter combinations in Θ, the problem can be expressed as:

$$\theta_n^* = \begin{cases} \theta_n & \text{if } WSD_C(\theta_n) > WSD_C(\theta_{n-1}) \\ \theta_{n-1} & \text{otherwise} \end{cases} \tag{4}$$

However, when the WSD system is probabilistic, there isn't a unique F-score given for a θ_n, but every evaluation of WSD_C may potentially return a different F-score value. Thus, WSD_C follows an unknown probability distribution X that depends on θ_n: $WSD_C(\theta_n) \sim X(\theta_n)$.

A sensible approach in this case would be to follow the model (Fig. 1b) proposed by (Painton and Diwekar, 1995), and to evaluate the objective function WSD_C several times and then consider the expected value as an estimator of the resulting distribution. However, even if the means are different, there is no guarantee the difference is not due to random chance.

The more general way to deal with this uncertainty about the statistical significance of the difference of expected values is to simply apply a standard statistical test in order to determine the significance level and decide whether or not to go ahead with the comparison. Another simpler approach, the one retained in fact, is to integrate into the scoring function a penalty factor that directly takes into account the variability of the distributions. This problem will specifically be addressed in more detail in Section 6.3.

6 Simulated Annealing

6.1 General Presentation

Simulated annealing is a stochastic combinatorial optimisation technique originally proposed by (Kirkpatrick et al., 1983). Given a function $f(\theta)$ that takes a vector of discrete parameters θ, Simulated

[1]From now on, the vector arrow will be omitted and $\vec{\theta}$ will be written as θ.

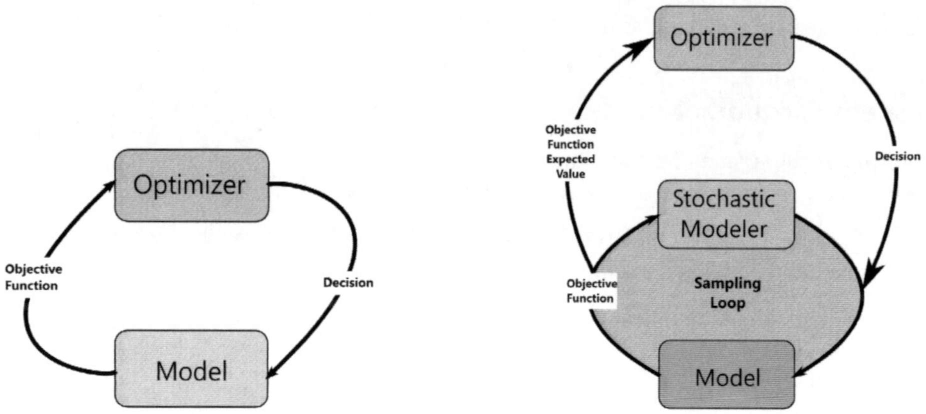

(a) Classical optimisation model (b) Stochastic optimisation model

Figure 1: Classical optimisation model versus stochastic optimisation model

Annealing aims at finding the combination of parameter that maximises or minimises that function. (Kirkpatrick et al., 1983) draw a parallel between statistical mechanics and combinatorial optimisation and apply ideas from the Metropolis-Hastings algorithm (Metropolis et al., 1953) (simulation of the behaviour of many body systems) to combinatorial optimisation.

The principle of Simulated annealing is to first start from an initial configuration (combination) of the function parameters θ_0 as well as an initial temperature T_0. The initial θ_0, is often chosen randomly, but putting an already good solution can accelerate the search.

Then, the algorithm iteratively applies a random change operator R to the current configuration in order to obtain a modified configuration $\theta^{'} = R(\theta)$.

The value of the modified configuration $f(\theta^{'})$ is compared to the value of the current configuration $f(\theta)$, such that $\Delta f = f(\theta^{'}) - f(\theta)$. An acceptance function $P(\Delta f)$ is then used to determine whether to keep the current configuration or to accept the modified configuration.

In the original SA algorithm, the acceptance function is expressed using the Metropolis criterion and the Boltzmann distribution as shown in Equation 5.

$$P(\Delta f) = \begin{cases} 1 & \text{if } \Delta f < 0 \\ exp\left(\frac{-\Delta f}{T}\right) & \text{otherwise} \end{cases} \tag{5}$$

With gradient descent or hill climbing search, only configuration that have a higher score are kept, while inferior configurations are systematically rejected. The problems with these approaches lies in the fact that complex functions often have many local minima and maxima, and the algorithm will likely converge on such a minimum or maximum.

Simulated Annealing, on the other hand, has a probability of accepting inferior configurations as a local minima/maxima escape strategy. The initial temperature is chosen so that at the beginning of the exploration, inferior configurations are almost always kept. After each iteration of the simulation, the temperature decreases and with it the probability to keep inferior configuration. As such, the algorithm starts with a wide and coarse exploration of the search space and then gradually converges on a fine grained exploration of a specific area around a minimum or maximum (hopefully close to the global minimum or maximum).

The convergence criterion for the algorithm can either be when the temperature reaches a threshold called *freezing* temperature or when the system is deemed to stabilize (usually a number of cycles during which improvements to the objective function are marginal or non-existent).

6.2 Cooling schedule and candidate generation

In SA, the way the temperature decreases is key to the performance of the algorithm. A logarithmic cooling schedule ($T_n = \frac{T_0}{ln(n)}$) is theoretically sufficient in order to guarantee convergence (Ingber, 1996), however, it is too slow for many problems. A more common cooling schedule is geometric $T_n = T_0 \cdot (\alpha)^n$, where alpha is the cooling factor. However, on the one hand the slope of the cooling curve will be very steep even for α close to one and on the other hand, the curve itself is convex. This means that the slope of the curve will get steep very fast, thus leading to a fast convergence at the cost of optimality.

For this reason, (Ingber, 1996) proposes in his Adaptive Simulated Annealing algorithm to use an inverse exponential cooling schedule that will decrease quickly at the start and then slow down. Such a schedule corresponds much better to combinatorial optimisation algorithms, where we want to start with a broad search (accepting many inferior configurations) and then focus on a specific area of the search space. (Ingber, 1996) proposed the expression in equations 6 and 7, which we adopted for our implementation. Here, m and n are two scaling factors that can be used to tune the schedule for specific problems.

$$T_k = T_0 \cdot exp\left(-c_i \cdot k^{\frac{1}{|\theta|}}\right) \tag{6}$$

$$c_i = m \cdot exp\left(\frac{-n}{D}\right) \tag{7}$$

Furthermore, the traditional SA, generates a new candidate configuration by uniformly selecting an index of the vector and by applying a random uniform change on the value, over the full range of possible values for that index. (Ingber, 1996) argues that once the system is colder, there is no point to explore the full range. Indeed, exploring an increasingly smaller neighbourhood as the temperature lowers and the systems converges on a specific area of the search space, allows an increase in computational efficiency while having no negative effects on the end result.

Equation 8 presents the probability distribution used for the candidate generation for each parameter, where $u_i \in U(0,1)$ is a uniform random number between 0 and 1.

$$y = sign\left(u - \frac{1}{2}\right) T_k \left[\left(1 + \frac{1}{T_k}\right)^{|2u-1|} - 1\right] \tag{8}$$

From there, the new value of a parameter $\theta^{(i)}$ of θ at iteration k can be determined with the expression in Equation 9 for a real parameter and Equation 10 for an integer parameter.

$$\theta_{k+1}^{(i)} = \theta_k^{(i)} + y(\theta_{max}^{(i)} - \theta_{min}^{(i)}) \tag{9}$$

$$\theta_{k+1}^{(i)} = \theta_k^{(i)} + \lfloor y(\theta_{max}^{(i)} - \theta_{min}^{(i)}) \rfloor \tag{10}$$

6.3 Handling uncertainty

As mentioned in Section 5, when dealing with an uncertain objective function, one needs to add an extra loop in the process, in order to generate samples from the evaluation of the objective function f and then to use the expected value as a global objective function.

For a given θ, we can build a list of samples $Ls(\theta) = \bigcup_{i=0}^{N}\{f(\theta)\}$ and then consider a modified objective function that uses the expected value of the sample distribution: $\Phi_E(\theta) = \overline{x_\theta}$, where $\overline{x_\theta} = \frac{1}{N} \cdot \sum_{x_i \in Ls(\theta)} x_i$. Then, Φ_E can be used directly instead of f as the global objective function.

6.4 Adaptive Penalty term

In order to deal with the variability of the distributions, (Painton and Diwekar, 1995) propose to add to the expression of Φ_E, a penalty factor based on the scaled standard deviation $\sigma_\theta = \sqrt{\frac{\sum_{x_i \in Ls(\theta)}(x_i - \overline{x_\theta})^2}{N}}$, weighted by a quantity that depends on the temperature. More specifically, their expression for Φ_E is:

$$\Phi_E(\theta) = \overline{x_\theta} + b(T) \cdot \frac{2 \cdot \sigma_\theta}{\sqrt{N}} \tag{11}$$

$$b(T) = \frac{b_0}{k^T} \tag{12}$$

Where b_0 is a small constant, k is a constant that represents the rate of increase of $b(T)$ and T the temperature of the system.

Given that at the beginning, the temperature is *high*, the search is wide into the search space. Thus, accepting non-significant changes has little adverse effect, although it leads to less evaluation of the objective function (which is costly to compute in principle).

6.5 Significance testing

In this article, we take a slightly different approach, by integrating a standard statistical test directly in the metropolis criterion, and by using Φ_E as only the expected value. Not only are such tests widely available in existing libraries, additionally, we avoid the hassle of adding two more constants to the estimation algorithm.

Depending on the properties of the distribution, different tests may be applied. The most widely used test for significance is the unpaired two-sample student t-test. However three important pre-requisites must be met before the test can be applied.

The distributions of samples in the groups must be normal, the samples in the groups must be independent, and the variances of the groups must be equal. In the case of simulated annealing under uncertainty, there is no guarantee that the distributions all keep these properties. Thus, in order to use the t-test (Press et al., 1988), ot would be required to test the hypotheses for every new re-sampling of the objective function. This could be achieved by applying the Shapiro–Wilk (Shapiro and Wilk, 1965) test to test the normality assumption and Levene's test (Levene, 1960) for the equality of variances.

In case the equality of variances criterion is not met, there is an alternative, Welch's t-test (Welch, 1947) that does not make that assumption. However, if the distribution is not normal, there is no other choice but to apply a non-parametric test.

A much simpler alternative, is to directly apply a non-parametric significance test, such as the Mann–Whitney U unpaired test, as there are no assumption about the distribution of the samples. The only requirement is that the values are ordinal and not regularly paced.

6.5.1 Modified Metropolis criterion

Since the objective function returns a numerical value, the Mann–Whitney U can be applied directly in the metropolis criterion as such:

$$P(\Delta f) = \begin{cases} 1 & \text{if } \Delta Phi_E < 0 \text{ and } p_\theta < \alpha \\ e^{\frac{-\Delta Phi_E}{T}} & \text{otherwise} \end{cases} \tag{13}$$

The test is based on the formulation of a null-hypothesis that states that the distribution of the two groups of samples are equal. Here, p_θ is the p-value (probability of true positives) resulting from the test and α a threshold. If the p-value is below the threshold, then we reject the null-hypothesis and conclude that the distributions must be different.

For example with $\alpha = 0.05$ the null-hypothesis will be rejected if the probability of having a type I error is more that 95%: in other words, $(1-p) > (1-\alpha)$.

The Mann–Whitney U (Mann and Whitney, 1947) is based on the comparison of the ranks of the samples within each group. The first step toward calculating the p-value is to group all the sample together, to sort them in ascending order, and to assign a rank to each value. From the respective ranks of the samples, can be computed R_θ, is the sum of ranks for $Ls(\theta)$ and $R_{\theta'}$ the sum of ranks for $Ls(\theta')$. Here, the number of samples for both groups are always equal to N.

6.5.2 Computing the p-value

From the sum of ranks, the U statistic can be computed as $U = min\left(R_\theta - \frac{N(N-1)}{2}; R_{\theta'} - \frac{N(N-1)}{2}\right) = min\left(R_\theta; R_{\bar{\theta'}}\right) - \frac{N(N-1)}{2}$.

For a sufficiently large N, the U statistic is an approximation of the normal distribution, and after applying a standardization by calculating the z statistic, the p-value can be retrieved from the probability density function of the normal distribution:

$$z = \frac{U - \overline{U}}{\sigma_U} \qquad \overline{U} = \frac{N^2}{2} \qquad \sigma_U = \sqrt{\frac{N^2(2N+1)}{12}} \qquad p_\theta = N(z, \overline{U}, \sigma_U) = \frac{1}{\sqrt{2\pi} \cdot \sigma_U} e^{-\frac{1}{2}\left(\frac{z-\overline{U}}{\sigma_U}\right)^2} \tag{14}$$

Despite the apparent complexity of the process of calculating and testing the p-value, the Mann–Whitney U test is rather standard and available in many libraries for various programming languages, including Java that we used for our implementation.

7 Experimental protocol

The principle used for the evaluation of the variant of simulated annealing considered for the estimation of parameters in an uncertain setting, was to consider the Semeval 2007 Task 7 annotated corpus. We split the corpus into a training and a test set in order to evaluate the parameter search with the Ant Colony Algorithm for WSD originally proposed in (Schwab and Guillaume, 2011) and then further improved upon in (Schwab et al., 2012). Furthermore, we want to determine exactly how much data was necessary to obtain a good set of parameter values.

Normally, in order to obtain a reliable training and thus parameters, it would be necessary to have a somewhat larger test set and to split it into several parts by randomly aggregating words to perform a $k-fold$ cross validation. However, the Ant Colony algorithm is meant to work on a full text as it exploits its structure. Notably, the order of the words and the continuity of sentences are very important. Making cross-validation sets randomly would thus only create a very noisy training data. Even just picking sentences at random still compromises the global coherence of the solutions found, and thus the parameters.

This is why we only considered a training on successively larger portions of our training corpus. More specifically, the experiments were carried out with 6,12,18,24,30 and 36 sentences in order from the first sentences to the full text in multiples of 6.

Furthermore, it is apparent that the nature of the training text itself has a big importance on the resulting parameters found. It is necessary to use a text that is as general as possible in terms of the senses it uses and of its theme as well as lexically varied. Even though, $k-fold$ cross validation cannot be applied directly in our experimental setting, we have decided to perform the experiment by taking, in turn, each text as a training corpus, with the remainder as a test corpus. Thus, we may also study the effect of the text itself and its characteristics (type of text, average polysemy, etc).

The implementation of this *uncertain* simulated annealing, runs the ant colony algorithm and passes the results through to the scorer to obtain the F-score values. For the stochastic loop, for every new candidate configuration, the ant colony algorithm is systematically run 50 times in order to guarantee a sufficient level of statistical significance. The search was left to converge for each successive number of sentences and then, each resulting parameter values were tested over 100 executions of the ant colony algorithm on the test corpus in order to ascertain the quality of the parameters.

The results for each number of sentences are evaluated with relation to both classical lesk baseline and the baseline obtained with the parameters before the estimation (BL). We used standard statistical tests to guarantee the statistical significance of the comparisons.

8 Experiments and Results

8.1 Initial parameter for the simulated annealing estimator

Before starting the experiment, it is important to select the parameters of the simulated annealing-based algorithm we are using. In total there are 4 parameters. k_{stb} the number of cycles with no accepted new configurations before the system is considered to have converged. T_0 the initial temperature, and m and n, the parameters of the cooling schedule. We are aware that the manual estimation of the parameters for the simulated annealing algorithm contradicts the general orientation of this paper, however one of the main reason simulated annealing was chosen is because its behaviour is well known and the parameters can be set heuristically quite effectively. Indeed a vast body of work covers the algorithm and can be used to guide the parameter estimation. The main idea is to use SA on algorithms with more complex and/or not so well understood parameter models. In fact, this process could be consider as a form of bootstrapping of sorts.

For the number of cycles before convergence, 20 is a good compromise between efficiency and optimality. As for n and m, we wanted to have a cooling schedule with the highest possible probability for subsequent iteration, while approaching 0 after 100 iterations. To this effect, after various experiments, we selected the values $n = -3$ and $m = 1$.

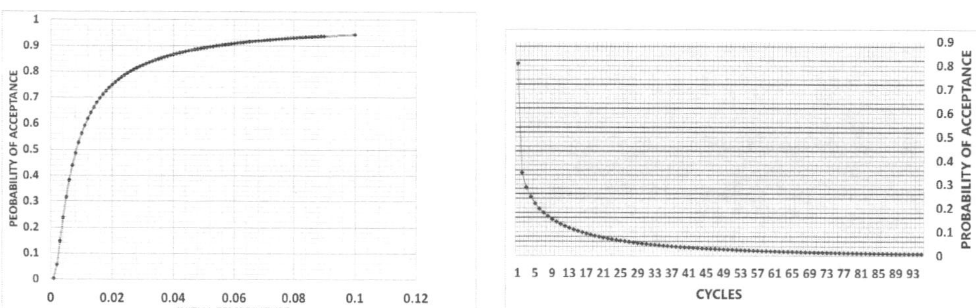

(a) Choice of the initial temperature (b) Cooling schedule acceptance probabilities

Figure 2: Classical optimisation model versus stochastic optimisation model

However, the most important parameter is the initial temperature, as it needs to be set to a certain level of probability of acceptance. Of course, since the probability of acceptance depends of the difference between successive scores, the first step toward selecting the initial temperature is to measure the average difference between successive scores. Therefore, it is necessary to run the algorithm while only sampling parameter configuration, without making any decisions about acceptance or convergence. Thus, we ran the algorithm this way and obtained an average F-score delta of **0.57%** with a standard deviation of 0.0047.

It is described in the literature that a good value for the initial acceptance probability is 0.8. Thus, to find the initial temperature, we can plot the graph of acceptance probability given the initial temperature (Figure 2a) by computing $e^{\frac{-0.58}{T_i}}$ with various values of T_i. Given that T is in the same unit as the objective function, the value must be situated between 0 and 1. In the present case, the value of T_i for which $e^{\frac{-0.58}{T_i}} = 0.8$ is **0.27**. After the parameters have been set, it is possible to directly plot the cooling schedule in terms of the average acceptance probabilities (Figure 2b) by using Equation 6.

8.2 Analysis

For each text used as a training set, we applied the standard Shapiro-Wilks (Shapiro and Wilk, 1965) non-normality test and the Levene's homoscedacity test (Levene, 1960) at a $\alpha = 0.1$ threshold, in order to verify the assumptions necessary to apply parametric statistical tests. For the results for Texts 1,2,3 the distributions resulting from each sentence led a to non-significant Shapiro Wilks, thus not allowing to reject the null hypothesis that the distributions are normal. Levene's test was significant for all texts, meaning that the variances are homogeneous. However for texts 4 and 5, the Shapiro-Wilks test was significant, thus making us reject the null hypothesis that the distributions are normal.

Thus, for text 1,2 and 3 we applied a standard Anova test and found a p-value that is also significant at the $\alpha = 0.01$ level. Furthermore we carried out the Tukey pairwise test, which significant differences in mean between most groups unless otherwise specified.

For texts 4 and 5 we applied the non-parametric rank-based Kruskal-Wallis test (**?**), which is similar to ANOVA for situations where the distributions involved are not normal. For the non parametric pair-wise test, we applied a non-parametric variant of Tukey's test, which the null hypothesis that "The probability of a sample from b being greater than a sample from a is superior to 0.5".

Table 3 and Figure 3a present the results for the first text as a training set in terms of value and in a graphical box plot representation.

We can see for the first text in Table 3 and Figure 3a that with only 6 sentences, the results obtained after the estimations are worse that with the original parameters by 4.01%. With 12 and 18 sentences, the obtained results start to at the level of the *Before* (BL on the graph) baseline. For 12 there is an improvement of 1.04% and for 18, a decrease of 0.42%. It appears that adding sentences is not necessarily positive, given that from 12 to 18 the results quality decreased.

Then, the results for 24, 30 and 36 are notably better than the *Before baseline* by 1.98%, 1.98% and 1.99% and close, yet still below to the First Sense baseline with 1.07% to 0.8%. However, after 24 sentences, there aren't any significant improvements by adding more sentences.

Sentences	$\overline{F_s}(\%)$	σ_{F_s}	Not Sign.	E_a	E_{max}	δ_ϕ	E_0	ω	L_v	δ_v
First Sense	77.59									
Before	74.54	0.54	∅	1	8	0.900	20	10	90	0.900
6	70.51	0.86	∅	1	2	0.650	10	5	90	0.360
12	75.58	0.69	∅	12	8	0.101	19	24	90	0.870
18	74.12	0.81	∅	7	9	0.457	20	19	78	0.900
24	76.52	0.38	30, 36	18	45	0.922	26	10	60	0.979
30	76.52	0.41	24, 36	11	20	0.903	11	8	40	0.927
36	76.53	0.38	24, 30	17	60	0.490	20	10	92	0.359

Table 3: Results in terms of the average F_{score} and its standard deviation σ_{F_s} for a given set of parameter values. Unless specified, the pairwise Tukey HSD test is significant with $\alpha = 0.01$.

As for the values of the parameters, only a few conjectures can be drawn. It appears first that the value of some parameters (L_v) have very little effect on the quality of the results, while others (E_a, E_max, E_0), have

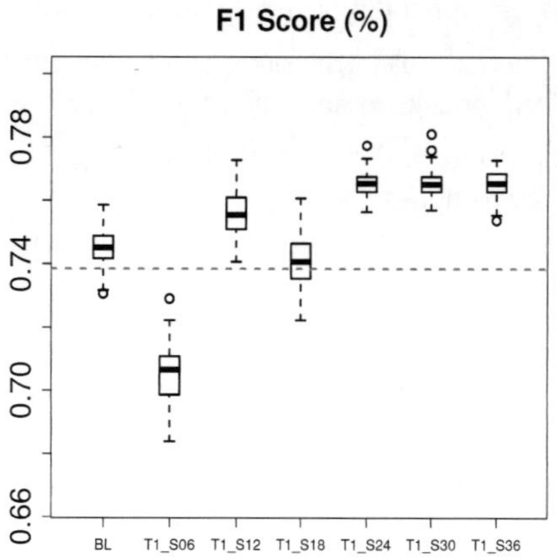

(a) Training on Text 1, Test on Texts 2,3,4,5

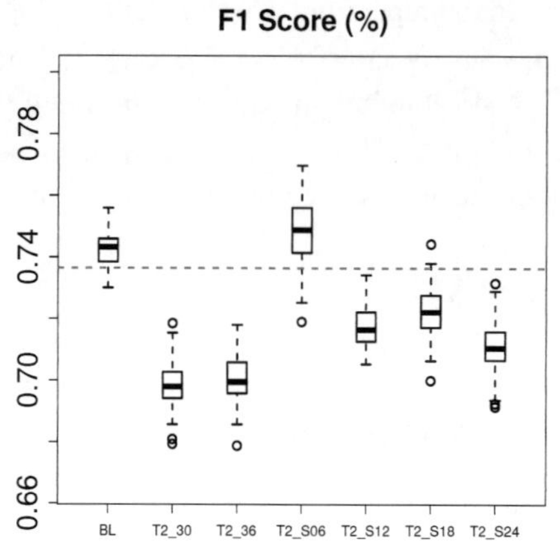

(b) Training on Text 2, Test on Texts 1,3,4,5

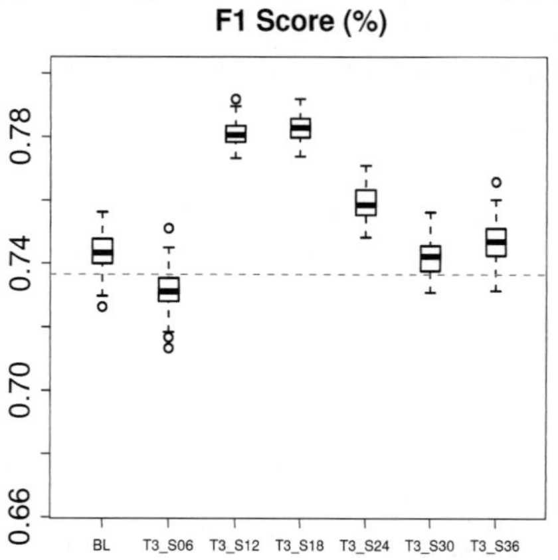

(c) Training on Text 3, Test on Texts 1,2,4,5

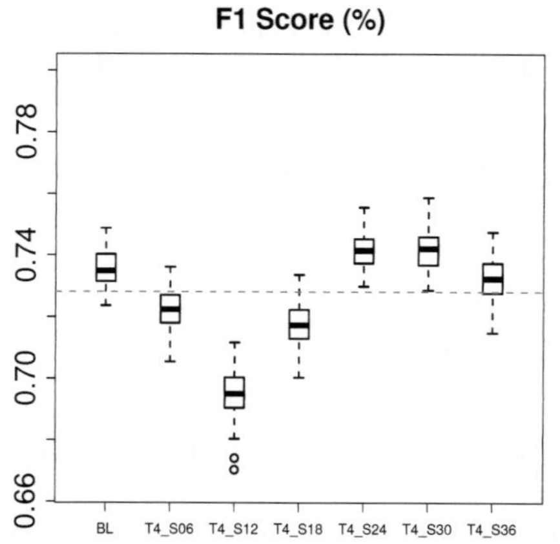

(d) Training on Text 4, Test on Texts 1,2,3,5

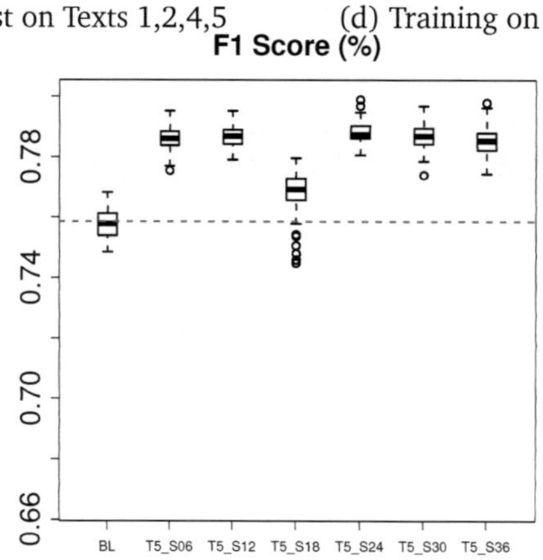

(e) Training on Text 5, Test on Texts 1,2,3,4

Figure 3: Box plots of the results for the training on Text 1 with different numbers of sentences compared to the Lesk algorithm 3(dashed line) and the Baseline of the parameters before the estimation.

Sentences	$\overline{F_s}(\%)$	σ_{F_s}	Not Sign.
Lesk	73.64		
Before	74.25	0.53	∅
6	74.86	0.74	∅
12	71.74	1.02	∅
18	72.27	0.65	∅
24	71.07	0.76	∅
30	69.81	0.53	36
36	70.06	0.70	30

(a) Results for Text 2 as a training corpus

Sentences	$\overline{F_s}(\%)$	σ_{F_s}	Not Sign.
Lesk	73.65		
Before	74.54	0.57	30
6	73.15	0.64	∅
12	78.10	0.37	18
18	78.25	0.38	12
24	78.89	0.53	∅
30	74.18	0.54	BL
36	74.67	0.68	∅

(b) Results for Text 3 as a training corpus

Sentences	$\overline{F_s}(\%)$	σ_{F_s}	Not Sign.
Lesk	72.80		
Before	73.57	0.57	∅
6	72.18	0.73	∅
12	69.46	0.79	∅
18	71.75	0.74	∅
24	74.16	0.59	30
30	74.19	0.66	24
36	73.22	0.69	∅

(c) Results for Text 4 as a training corpus

Sentences	$\overline{F_s}(\%)$	σ_{F_s}	Not Sign.
Lesk	75.85		
Before	75.77	0.52	∅
6	76.60	0.37	12,24,30,36
12	78.68	0.33	24,30
18	76.86	0.69	∅
24	78.79	0.34	6,12,30
30	78.66	0.37	6,12,24,36
36	78.53	0.44	6,30

(d) Results for Text 5 as a training corpus

Table 4: Results in terms of the average F_{score} and its standard deviation σ_{F_s} for the parameters found with each number of sentences of training data.

a profound effect. We can observe that for all three number of sentences 24, 30, 36, we systematically have: $E_a < E_{max}$, $E_a \leq E_0$ and finally $\delta_\phi \simeq \delta_v$. Given that for the number of sentences 24, 30 and 36 the distribution are almost equal, we can hypothesise that there are to some degrees equivalences between some parameter value combinations.

We are also interested in the effect of the number of sentences by using the other texts of the corpus as training data. Furthermore we want to evaluate the fitness of certain types of texts for the purposes of parameter estimation for WSD. Tables 4a, 4b, 4c and 4d present the results for Texts 2,3,4,5 respectively as training sets. We will not, for these texts do a detailed analysis of the parameter values found, but will only look at the general trends with relation to the number of sentences and the properties of the texts. Figures 3b,3c,3d and 3e present box plots of the resulting score distributions for each text.

It is apparent that the quality of the parameter estimation widely depends on the nature of the texts used, as well as the quantity of data used for the training. For text 2, the results with any more than 6 sentences are all below the Lesk baseline, which could be indicative of a few general introductory sentences followed by very specific vocabulary. Text two is in fact an extract from the Wall Street Journal summarising a public scandal using very specific terms.

There are other cases, such as for text 3, where over fitting occurs very rapidly as the number of sentences increases. Such a behaviour could be explained by latter sentences of the text being domain specific and detrimental to the generality of the training. We observe a similar behaviour with text 4 towards the middle of the text. Text 3 is an extract from the wall street journal and is about a journalism convention, whereas Text 4 is a Wikipedia article about computer programming.

Text 5, a literary text extracted from a book, features the most steady training material, Indeed, except with 18 sentences, the resulting distributions from the estimated parameters are roughly equivalent as indicated by the non-significant differences. The results are about at the same distance above the Lesk baseline than in Text 1 with 24 sentences and above. Such a text would be very desirable for parameter training, as even little data is enough to obtain a very general training.

While it is not possible to make use of cross validation by taking random sentences, it may be a future possibility to take chunks of texts containing several sentences unified thematically or semantically for example and that have good training properties. Thus making a more formal cross-validation possible and allow to find the best combination of sentences for the purposes of parameter estimation with more systematic criteria.

9 Conclusions and Perspectives

We have presented and evaluated a variant of simulated annealing for uncertain cost functions. More specifically, we have adapted the work of (Painton and Diwekar, 1995) to use standard statistical tests, as well as integrated some elements of adaptivity inspired by (Ingber, 1996)'s Adaptive Simulated Annealing. We performed experiments on Semeval 2007 task 7 and found that the quality of the results from a given set of estimated parameters very much depend on the nature of the text. However, from the texts in our corpus it appears that very general texts with a diverse yet non domain specific lexicon are the best choice for the estimation of parameters. As exhibited for one of the texts, even very small training sets are sufficient to obtain good results granted the text has the right properties.

For future work concerning this parameter estimation approach, we are planning some more thorough experiments involving the other texts, as well parts of SemCor. Furthermore, there are many potential ways to improve the parameter search algorithm, notably through the integration of more adaptive elements from Adaptive Simulated Annealing. Furthermore, it may be beneficial to evaluate a variant where the statistical test is integrated in the objective function as a penalty term, like (Painton and Diwekar, 1995) propose with the standard deviation.

Furthermore, it would be very interesting to adapt our approach to perform joint optimisation of features and parameters as done in (Daelemans et al., 2003), even though the stochastic aspect would make it a much lengthier process in order to ensure statistically valid results.

Resources and programs

The implementations of both the parameter estimation and the Ant Colony Algorithm are both available online as Free Software under the GNU Lesser General Public License: `https://forge.imag.fr/projects/formica/`. More information is available on the WSD page of our research group: `http://getalp.imag.fr/xwiki/bin/view/WSD/`.

Funding

This research was funded by the French Ministry Research Allocation and by the Traouiero ANR project.

References

Bolhasani (2004). Parameter estimation of vehicle handling model using genetic algorithm. 11(1-2):121–127.

Cowie, J., Guthrie, J., and Guthrie, L. (1992). Lexical disambiguation using simulated annealing. In *COLING '92*, pages 359–365, Nantes, France. ACL.

Daelemans, W., Hoste, V., Meulder, F. D., and Naudts, B. (2003). Combined optimization of feature selection and algorithm parameters in machine learning of language. In *In Proc of the 14th European Conference on Machine Learning, ECML 2003*, pages 84–95, Cavtat-Dubrovnik, Croatia.

Decadt, B., Hoste, V., Daelemans, W., and Van den Bosch, A. (2004). Gambl, genetic algorithm optimization of memory-based wsd. In Mihalcea, R. and Edmonds, P., editors, *Senseval-3: Third International*

Workshop on the Evaluation of Systems for the Semantic Analysis of Text, pages 108–112, Barcelona, Spain. Association for Computational Linguistics.

Gelbukh, A., Sidorov, G., and Han, S.-Y. (2003). Evolutionary approach to natural language Word Sense Disambiguation through global coherence optimization. *WSEAS Transactions on Communications*, 1(2):11–19.

Goutte, C. and Gaussier, E. (2005). A probabilistic interpretation of precision, recall and f-score, with implication for evaluation. In *ECIR 27th European Conference on Information Retrieva*, Santiago de Compostela, Spain.

Ingber, L. (1996). Adaptive simulated annealing (asa): Lessons learned. *Control and Cybernetics*, 25(1):33–54.

Katare, S., Bhan, A., Caruthers, J. M., Delgass, W. N., and Venkatasubramanian, V. (2004). A hybrid genetic algorithm for efficient parameter estimation of large kinetic models. *Computers & Chemical Engineering*, 28(12):2569 – 2581.

Kay, S. M. (1993). *Fundamentals of statistical signal processing: estimation theory*. Prentice-Hall, Inc., Upper Saddle River, NJ, USA.

Kim, K.-J. and Diwekar, U. M. (2002). Efficient combinatorial optimization under uncertainty. 1. algorithmic development. 41(5):1276–1284.

Kirkpatrick, S., Gelatt, C. D., and Vecchi, M. P. (1983). Optimization by simulated annealing. *Science*, 220(4598):671–680.

Lee, Y. H., Park, S. K., and Chang, D.-E. (2006). Parameter estimation using the genetic algorithm and its impact on quantitative precipitation forecast. *Annales Geophysicae*, 24:3185–3189.

Levene, H. (1960). Robust tests for equality of variances. In *Ingram Olkin, Harold Hotelling, et alia.*, pages 278–292. Stanford University Press.

Mann, H. B. and Whitney, D. R. (1947). On a Test of Whether one of Two Random Variables is Stochastically Larger than the Other. *The Annals of Mathematical Statistics*, 18(1):50–60.

Metropolis, N., Rosenbluth, A. W., Rosenbluth, M. N., Teller, A. H., and Teller, E. (1953). Equation of state calculations by fast computing machines. *The Journal of Chemical Physics*, 21(6):1087–1092.

Painton, L. and Diwekar, U. (1995). Stochastic annealing for synthesis under uncertainty. *European Journal of Operational Research*, 83(3):489 – 502.

Pan, Z., Chen, Y., Kang, L., and Zhang, Y. (1995). Parameter estimation by genetic algorithms for nonlinear regression. In *in G.Z.Liu (Ed.), Optimization Techniques and Applications, Proceedings of International Conference on Optimization Technique and Applications '95*, pages 946–953.

Paterakis, E., Petridis, V., and Kehagias, A. (1998). Genetic algorithm in parameter estimation of nonlinear dynamic systems. In *Proceedings of the 5th International Conference on Parallel Problem Solving from Nature*, PPSN V, pages 1008–1017, London, UK, UK. Springer-Verlag.

Press, W. H., Flannery, B. P., Teukolsky, S. A., and Vetterling, W. T. (1988). *Numerical recipes in C: the art of scientific computing*. Cambridge University Press, New York, NY, USA.

Schwab, D., Goulian, J., Tchechmedjiev, A., and Blanchon, H. (2012). Ant colony algorithm for the unsupervised word sense disambiguation of texts: Comparison and evaluation. To be published.

Schwab, D. and Guillaume, N. (2011). A global ant colony algorithm for word sense disambiguation based on semantic relatedness. In *Highlights in Practical Applications of Agents and Multiagent Systems*, volume 89 of *Advances in Intelligent and Soft Computing*, pages 257–264. Springer Berlin / Heidelberg.

Shapiro, S. S. and Wilk, M. B. (1965). An analysis of variance test for normality (complete samples). *Biometrika*, 52(3/4):591–611.

Sharman, K. and McClurkin, G. (1989). Genetic algorithms for maximum likelihood parameter estimation. In *Acoustics, Speech, and Signal Processing, 1989. ICASSP-89., 1989 International Conference on*, pages 2716 –2719 vol.4.

Veronis, J. and Ide, N. M. (1990). Word sense disambiguation with very large neural networks extracted from machine readable dictionaries. In *Proceedings of the 13th conference on Computational linguistics - Volume 2*, COLING '90, pages 389–394, Stroudsburg, PA, USA. Association for Computational Linguistics.

Welch, B. L. (1947). The Generalization of 'Student's' Problem when Several Different Population Variances are Involved. *Biometrika*, 34(1/2):28–35.

Yao, L. and Sethares, W. (1994). Nonlinear parameter estimation via the genetic algorithm. *Signal Processing, IEEE Transactions on*, 42(4):927 –935.

Author Index

Association for Computational Linguistics
209 N. Eighth Street
Stroudsburg, Pennsylvania 18360

CURRAN ASSOCIATES INC
proceedings
.com

2nd Workshop on Sentiment Analysis Where AI Meets Psychology

(SAAIP 2012)

Held at the 24th International Conference on Computational Linguistics (COLING 2012)

Mumbai, India
15 December 2012

ISBN: 978-1-62748-354-4